Mastering
IT Infrastructure Management
Concepts, Techniques, and Applications

Nikhilesh Mishra,
Author

Website
https://www.nikhileshmishra.com

Copyright Information

Dedication

This book is lovingly dedicated to the cherished memory of my father, **Late Krishna Gopal Mishra**, and my mother**, Mrs. Vijay Kanti Mishra.** Their unwavering support, guidance, and love continue to inspire me.

Table of Contents

COPYRIGHT INFORMATION   I

DEDICATION   II

TABLE OF CONTENTS   III

AUTHOR'S PREFACE   VIII

CHAPTER 1   1

Introduction to IT Infrastructure Management   1
    A.   Definition and Significance of IT Infrastructure Management   2
    B.   Historical Evolution of IT Infrastructure   5
    C.   The Role of IT Infrastructure in Modern Organizations   9
    D.   Benefits of IT Infrastructure Management   13
    E.   Setting Objectives for Effective Infrastructure Management   18

CHAPTER 2   24

Introduction to IT Infrastructure Components   24
    A.   Data Centers and Their Role in Infrastructure   24
    B.   Hardware Infrastructure (Servers, Networking, Storage)   29
    C.   Software Infrastructure (Operating Systems, Virtualization)   33
    D.   Network Architecture (LAN, WAN, VPN)   38
    E.   Emerging Technologies in Infrastructure   42

CHAPTER 3   48

IT Infrastructure Planning and Design   48
    A.   Capacity Planning in IT Infrastructure   48
    B.   Scalability and Redundancy in IT Infrastructure   53
    C.   Disaster Recovery and Business Continuity in IT Infrastructure   58
    D.   Security Considerations in IT Infrastructure   64
    E.   Cost Estimation and Budgeting in IT Infrastructure   69

CHAPTER 4   **75**

IT Service Management (ITSM)   **75**
    A.   ITIL Framework and Best Practices in IT Service Management (ITSM) 75
    B.   Service Catalog Management in IT Service Management (ITSM)   81
    C.   Incident, Problem, and Change Management in IT Service Management
(ITSM)   86
    D.   Service Desk Operations in IT Service Management (ITSM)   92
    E.   Key Performance Indicators (KPIs) in IT Service Management (ITSM) 97

CHAPTER 5   **104**

Infrastructure as Code (IaC) and Automation   **104**
    A.   Understanding Infrastructure as Code (IaC) Principles   104
    B.   Tools and Technologies for Infrastructure as Code (IaC)   109
    C.   Automation in IT Infrastructure Management   114
    D.   Continuous Integration and Continuous Deployment (CI/CD)   119
    E.   Benefits of Infrastructure as Code (IaC) and Automation   124

CHAPTER 6   **130**

Networking and Data Center Setup   **130**
    A.   Selecting the Right Location for Networking and Data Center Setup   130
    B.   Power and Cooling Requirements for Networking and Data Center Setup
      135
    C.   Rack Layout and Design in Data Center Setup   140
    D.   Server Hardware Setup in Data Center   144
    E.   Network Infrastructure in Data Center Setup   149
    F.   Cabling and Cable Management in Data Center Setup   154
    G.   Storage Solutions in Data Center Setup   160
    H.   Redundancy and High Availability in Data Center Setup   165
    I.   Data Center Operations: Ensuring Efficient and Reliable Infrastructure
Management   170
    J.   Security Measures in Data Center Operations   176
    K.   Scalability and Growth in Data Center Operations   181
    L.   Documentation and Asset Management in Data Center Operations   187

CHAPTER 7   **193**

Cabling, Crimping, and Hardware Installation   **193**
    A.   Types of Cabling in IT Infrastructure: Ethernet, Fiber Optic, and More
      194
    B.   Cable Routing and Organization in IT Infrastructure   199
    C.   Crimping and Termination Techniques in IT Infrastructure   204

D.   Best Practices for Hardware Installation in IT Infrastructure   209

CHAPTER 8   **215**

Data Center Setup and Configuration   **215**
A.   Initial Data Center Planning: The Foundation of a Robust Infrastructure
216
B.   Layout and Design Considerations for Data Centers   221
C.   Installation of Racks and Hardware in Data Centers   225
D.   Power and Cooling Infrastructure in Data Centers: Ensuring Efficiency
and Reliability   230
E.   Network Infrastructure Setup: Building a Solid Foundation for Data
Center Connectivity   235
F.   Security Measures for Data Centers: Safeguarding the Digital Fortress 240
G.   Documentation and Asset Management for Data Centers: The Foundation
of Operational Excellence   244

CHAPTER 9   **250**

Cloud Infrastructure Management: Navigating the Digital Skyline   **250**
A.   Cloud Service Models (IaaS, PaaS, SaaS): Unveiling the Layers of Cloud
Computing   251
B.   Cloud Deployment Models (Public, Private, Hybrid): Navigating the
Cloud Landscape   255
C.   Managing Multi-Cloud Environments: Orchestrating the Cloud
Symphony   260
D.   Cost Optimization in the Cloud: Maximizing Efficiency and Value   264
E.   Cloud Security and Compliance: Safeguarding Your Digital Assets   269

CHAPTER 10   **274**

Storage and Data Management: Navigating the Digital Data Seas   **274**
A.   Data Storage Technologies (SAN, NAS, Object Storage): Building the
Foundation of Data Management   275
B.   Data Backup and Recovery: Safeguarding Business Continuity   279
C.   Data Lifecycle Management: Maximizing the Value of Data from Birth to
Retirement   284
D.   Big Data and Analytics Infrastructure: Fueling Data-Driven Insights 288
E.   Data Governance and Compliance: Upholding Data Integrity and Legal
Standards   294

CHAPTER 11   **299**

Virtualization and Containerization: Unleashing the Power of Resource Efficiency   **299**
    A.   Virtualization Technologies: Unlocking Efficiency and Flexibility with VMware and Hyper-V   302
    B.   Containerization: Revolutionizing Software Deployment with Docker and Kubernetes   307
    C.   Microservices Architecture: Building Scalable and Agile Software Ecosystems   311
    D.   Orchestrating Containers: Streamlining Deployment and Management with Kubernetes   316
    E.   Container Security and Management: Safeguarding Containerized Applications   321

CHAPTER 12   **327**

Advanced Security Measures: Fortifying Your Digital Defenses   **327**
    A.   Intrusion Detection Systems (IDS): Fortifying Your Digital Perimeter 327
    B.   Penetration Testing: Probing for Security Weaknesses   332
    C.   Advanced Threat Mitigation: Defending Against Evolving Cyber Threats 337

CHAPTER 13   **343**

Hybrid Cloud and Multi-Cloud Management: Navigating the Future of Cloud Computing   **343**
    A.   Strategies for Hybrid Cloud Deployments: Bridging On-Premises and Cloud Worlds   343
    B.   Challenges of Multi-Cloud Management: Navigating Complexity in a Multi-Cloud World   348

CHAPTER 14   **353**

DevOps Integration: Bridging the Gap Between Development and Operations   **353**
    A.   DevOps Principles and Practices: Cultivating Collaboration for Efficient Software Delivery   353
    B.   Automation and Collaboration in DevOps: Streamlining Efficiency and Accelerating Software Delivery   358
    C.   DevOps Agility in Infrastructure Management: Paving the Way for Dynamic IT Operations   363

CHAPTER 15   **368**

Comprehensive Case Studies: Real-World Insights into IT Infrastructure Management   **368**
    A.   Real-world Examples of Effective IT Infrastructure Management: Learning from Success Stories   368
    B.   Industry-specific Case Studies: Tailoring IT Infrastructure Management for Success   373
    C.   Challenges Faced and Overcome in IT Infrastructure Management   378

CONCLUSION   384

RECAP OF KEY TAKEAWAYS   386

THE FUTURE OF IT INFRASTRUCTURE MANAGEMENT   393

GLOSSARY OF TERMS   398

RESOURCES AND REFERENCES   404

ACKNOWLEDGMENTS   406

ABOUT THE AUTHOR   408

Author's Preface

Welcome to the captivating world of the knowledge we are about to explore! Within these pages, we invite you to embark on a journey that delves into the frontiers of information and understanding.

Charting the Path to Knowledge

Dive deep into the subjects we are about to explore as we unravel the intricate threads of innovation, creativity, and problem-solving. Whether you're a curious enthusiast, a seasoned professional, or an eager learner, this book serves as your gateway to gaining a deeper understanding.

Your Guiding Light

From the foundational principles of our chosen field to the advanced frontiers of its applications, we've meticulously crafted this book to be your trusted companion. Each chapter is an expedition, guided by expertise and filled with practical insights to empower you on your quest for knowledge.

What Awaits You

- **Illuminate the Origins:** Embark on a journey through the historical evolution of our chosen field, discovering key milestones that have paved the way for breakthroughs.

- **Demystify Complex Concepts:** Grasp the fundamental principles, navigate intricate concepts, and explore practical applications.

- **Mastery of the Craft:** Equip yourself with the skills and knowledge needed to excel in our chosen domain.

Your Journey Begins Here

As we embark on this enlightening journey together, remember that mastery is not just about knowledge but also the wisdom to apply it. Let each chapter be a stepping stone towards unlocking your potential, and let this book be your guide to becoming a true connoisseur of our chosen field.

So, turn the page, delve into the chapters, and immerse yourself in the world of knowledge. Let curiosity be your compass, and let the pursuit of understanding be your guide.

Begin your expedition now. Your quest for mastery awaits!

Sincerely,

Nikhilesh Mishra,

Author

CHAPTER 1

Introduction to IT Infrastructure Management

In today's rapidly evolving technological landscape, the seamless operation of an organization's IT infrastructure has become not just a necessity but a strategic imperative. IT infrastructure forms the backbone of modern enterprises, facilitating the flow of data, the deployment of critical services, and the support of business operations. Understanding, optimizing, and effectively managing this complex ecosystem is the essence of IT Infrastructure Management.

This introduction sets the stage for a journey into the world of IT Infrastructure Management, where we will explore the significance of IT infrastructure, its historical evolution, its role in modern organizations, and the benefits and challenges associated with its management. As we delve deeper into this discipline, we will uncover the key components that make up an IT infrastructure, from data centers and hardware to software and network architecture, all of which play pivotal roles in ensuring the reliability, scalability, and security of an organization's technology foundation.

Join us as we embark on a comprehensive exploration of IT Infrastructure Management, uncovering the best practices, tools, and strategies that empower organizations to harness the full potential of their IT resources while navigating the ever-changing landscape of technology. Whether you're an IT professional seeking to enhance your skills or a business leader looking to optimize your organization's technology investments, this journey will provide you with valuable insights and knowledge to excel in the world of IT infrastructure management.

A. Definition and Significance of IT Infrastructure Management

In today's digital age, where technology is the driving force behind nearly every aspect of business and daily life, the effective management of IT infrastructure has emerged as a critical function for organizations of all sizes and industries. To understand the true significance of IT Infrastructure Management, it's essential to delve into its definition, explore its components, and recognize why it stands at the core of modern business operations.

Definition of IT Infrastructure Management

IT Infrastructure Management refers to the systematic process of planning, designing, implementing, and maintaining the technology components and resources necessary to support an organization's daily operations. It encompasses a wide array of elements, including hardware, software, data centers, networks, and various related services. At its core, IT Infrastructure Management aims to ensure that an organization's technology assets are reliable, efficient, secure, and aligned with its strategic goals.

The management of IT infrastructure involves a range of tasks and responsibilities, such as monitoring system performance, addressing issues and outages, optimizing resource utilization, implementing security measures, and planning for future growth and scalability. It is a multifaceted discipline that requires a blend of technical expertise, strategic thinking, and operational excellence.

The Significance of IT Infrastructure Management

1. **Business Continuity and Productivity:** IT infrastructure serves as the foundation upon which businesses operate in the digital age. Effective infrastructure management ensures high availability and minimizes downtime, allowing organizations to maintain productivity and deliver uninterrupted services to customers.

2. **Data Integrity and Security:** In an era where data is often a company's most valuable asset, IT Infrastructure Management plays a vital role in safeguarding sensitive information. This includes implementing robust security measures, such as firewalls, encryption, and access controls, to protect against

cyber threats and data breaches.

3. **Resource Optimization:** Efficient infrastructure management optimizes the utilization of resources, such as servers, storage, and network bandwidth. This leads to cost savings by reducing over-provisioning and ensuring that resources are allocated where they are needed most.

4. **Scalability and Adaptability:** A well-managed IT infrastructure is flexible and scalable, allowing organizations to adapt to changing business needs and growth requirements. Whether it's expanding to accommodate increased demand or scaling down during quieter periods, infrastructure management ensures the agility to respond effectively.

5. **Cost Control:** By monitoring and controlling IT expenditures, infrastructure management helps organizations manage their IT budgets effectively. This includes cost estimation, budgeting, and identifying opportunities for cost optimization.

6. **Compliance and Regulation:** Many industries are subject to specific regulations regarding data handling and security. IT Infrastructure Management assists in ensuring compliance with these regulations, reducing the risk of legal and financial consequences.

7. **Innovation and Competitive Advantage:** Effective infrastructure management frees up IT teams from routine

tasks, allowing them to focus on innovation and strategic initiatives. This can provide a competitive edge by enabling the rapid adoption of new technologies and business practices.

8. **Enhanced User Experience:** A well-managed IT infrastructure leads to a better user experience for both employees and customers. Faster response times, minimal disruptions, and seamless access to services contribute to overall satisfaction.

In conclusion, IT Infrastructure Management is not merely a support function within an organization; it is a strategic enabler of business success. Its significance lies in its ability to ensure the availability, reliability, and security of technology resources, ultimately contributing to improved efficiency, innovation, and competitiveness. As technology continues to advance, the role of IT Infrastructure Management will only grow in importance, making it an indispensable aspect of modern business operations.

B. Historical Evolution of IT Infrastructure

The historical evolution of IT infrastructure is a fascinating journey that reflects the ever-accelerating pace of technological advancement and its profound impact on the way businesses and individuals operate. To understand this evolution, it's essential to trace the key milestones and transformations that have shaped the IT infrastructure landscape over the years.

Mastering IT Infrastructure Management

1. Early Computing and Mainframes (1950s-1960s):

- The origins of IT infrastructure can be traced back to the development of early computers, such as the UNIVAC and IBM 701, in the 1950s.

- During this era, computing was largely centralized, with massive mainframe computers serving as the backbone of organizations. These mainframes required dedicated rooms and specialized personnel to operate.

- IT infrastructure primarily consisted of hardware, with little emphasis on software or networking.

2. Emergence of Mini-Computers (1960s-1970s):

- The 1960s and 1970s saw the advent of mini-computers, which were smaller and more affordable than mainframes. Companies like Digital Equipment Corporation (DEC) played a significant role in this development.

- Mini-computers brought computing power to smaller organizations and departments within larger enterprises, decentralizing IT infrastructure to some extent.

3. Rise of Personal Computers (1980s-1990s):

- The 1980s witnessed the proliferation of personal computers (PCs), thanks to companies like IBM, Apple, and Microsoft.

- PCs revolutionized IT infrastructure by placing computing power on the desks of individuals and enabling local processing and data storage.

- Local area networks (LANs) and client-server architecture started gaining prominence during this period.

4. Client-Server Computing (1990s-2000s):

- The 1990s marked the era of client-server computing, where organizations adopted networked environments with centralized servers and distributed client machines.

- IT infrastructure expanded to include networking components like routers, switches, and cabling, in addition to servers and PCs.

- The World Wide Web and the Internet became accessible to the public, leading to a global networked infrastructure.

5. Virtualization and Data Centers (2000s-Present):

- The 2000s brought virtualization technologies, such as VMware, which allowed multiple virtual servers to run on a single physical machine.

- Data centers evolved to house racks of servers, storage systems, and networking equipment. Cloud computing providers like Amazon Web Services (AWS) and Microsoft

Azure emerged.

- IT infrastructure became more scalable, flexible, and responsive, with the ability to provision resources on-demand.

6. Cloud Computing and Edge Computing (2010s-Present):

- Cloud computing revolutionized IT infrastructure further, enabling organizations to outsource their infrastructure needs to cloud providers.

- Edge computing emerged to bring processing closer to the source of data, enabling real-time analytics and reducing latency.

- Automation and Infrastructure as Code (IaC) became integral to managing and provisioning infrastructure resources.

7. Internet of Things (IoT) and 5G (Present and Future):

- The present and future of IT infrastructure are heavily influenced by the proliferation of IoT devices and the rollout of 5G networks.

- IT infrastructure must now accommodate the massive influx of data generated by IoT devices and support the low-latency requirements of 5G applications.

8. Artificial Intelligence (AI) and Quantum Computing (Emerging Trends):

- AI and machine learning are reshaping IT infrastructure by demanding powerful computational resources for training and inference.

- Quantum computing, although in its infancy, promises to disrupt traditional IT infrastructure with its potential to solve complex problems exponentially faster.

In conclusion, the historical evolution of IT infrastructure underscores the transformative power of technology. It has evolved from room-sized mainframes to highly distributed and virtualized environments, all while becoming an essential component of modern life and business operations. As technology continues to advance, IT infrastructure will undoubtedly continue to adapt and evolve to meet the changing needs of the digital age.

C. The Role of IT Infrastructure in Modern Organizations

In the digital age, information technology (IT) infrastructure is the backbone of modern organizations, irrespective of their size or industry. The role it plays is nothing short of transformative, impacting every facet of business operations, innovation, customer engagement, and competitiveness. To understand the profound significance of IT infrastructure in modern organizations, let's delve into its multifaceted roles.

1. Enabler of Business Operations:

- IT infrastructure provides the essential tools and resources for day-to-day business operations. This includes email systems, collaboration platforms, document management, and communication tools that enable employees to work efficiently and cohesively.

- Enterprise resource planning (ERP) systems, customer relationship management (CRM) software, and supply chain management solutions depend on robust IT infrastructure to manage and optimize various processes.

2. Facilitator of Digital Transformation:

- Modern organizations are undergoing digital transformations to remain competitive and meet the evolving needs of their customers. IT infrastructure is the enabler of this transformation, supporting the adoption of new technologies, such as cloud computing, AI, and IoT.

- Through IT infrastructure, organizations can collect, analyze, and act upon data, leading to data-driven decision-making and innovation.

3. Enhancer of Customer Engagement:

- The digital era has redefined customer engagement. IT infrastructure supports customer relationship management systems, e-commerce platforms, and omnichannel communication, allowing organizations to engage with customers in real-time and on their preferred channels.

- Customer data analytics, powered by IT infrastructure, enables personalization and tailored marketing strategies.

4. Guardian of Data and Security:

- In a world of increasing cyber threats and data breaches, IT infrastructure plays a critical role in safeguarding sensitive information. Firewalls, intrusion detection systems, encryption, and access controls are integral components.

- Backup and disaster recovery solutions ensure business continuity in the face of unforeseen disruptions.

5. Catalyst for Innovation and Agility:

- IT infrastructure empowers organizations to innovate rapidly. Cloud computing platforms, for instance, allow businesses to experiment with new services and scale resources as needed without significant upfront investments.

- Infrastructure as Code (IaC) and automation facilitate agility by enabling the rapid deployment and scaling of infrastructure resources.

6. Supporter of Remote and Flexible Work:

- The COVID-19 pandemic accelerated the shift toward remote work, highlighting the importance of IT infrastructure. Cloud-based collaboration tools, virtual private networks (VPNs), and secure access to company resources became essential for remote workforces.

- IT infrastructure ensures that employees can access critical data and applications securely from anywhere.

7. Driver of Cost Efficiency:

- Well-managed IT infrastructure optimizes resource utilization, reducing operational costs. Server virtualization, for example, allows multiple virtual servers to run on a single physical machine, minimizing hardware expenses.

- Cloud services offer cost-effective pay-as-you-go models, eliminating the need for extensive on-premises infrastructure.

8. Support for Compliance and Reporting:

- Regulatory compliance is a significant concern for many organizations. IT infrastructure plays a role in data governance, audit trails, and reporting, helping organizations meet legal and industry-specific requirements.

9. Contributor to Sustainability:

- IT infrastructure can promote sustainability efforts. Virtualization and cloud computing can lead to reduced energy consumption and a smaller carbon footprint compared to traditional data centers.

In conclusion, the role of IT infrastructure in modern organizations is nothing less than transformative. It is the linchpin that connects people, processes, and technologies, enabling businesses to thrive in an increasingly digital world. Its multifaceted role encompasses everything from supporting daily operations to driving innovation, safeguarding data, enhancing customer engagement, and ensuring business continuity. As technology continues to advance, the importance of IT infrastructure will only grow, making it a strategic imperative for organizations seeking long-term success.

D. Benefits of IT Infrastructure Management

Effective IT Infrastructure Management brings a multitude of benefits to organizations, enhancing their operational efficiency, competitiveness, and ability to adapt to a rapidly changing technological landscape. Here are some of the key benefits:

1. Improved Reliability and Availability:

- IT infrastructure management ensures that systems and services are highly available and reliable, minimizing downtime and disruptions. This leads to improved business continuity and customer satisfaction.

2. Enhanced Security:

- Proper management includes robust security measures, safeguarding critical data and systems from cyber threats. Regular security updates and monitoring help in identifying and mitigating vulnerabilities.

3. Optimal Resource Utilization:

- Infrastructure management ensures efficient allocation and utilization of resources like servers, storage, and network bandwidth. This optimization results in cost savings by reducing over-provisioning.

4. Scalability and Flexibility:

- Well-managed infrastructure is scalable, allowing organizations to expand or contract resources as needed. This adaptability is crucial in meeting changing business demands.

5. Cost Control and Efficiency:

- Effective management helps control IT costs by budgeting

accurately, optimizing resource use, and reducing operational inefficiencies. It prevents unnecessary expenditures and ensures a favorable return on investment.

6. Streamlined Operations:

- Automation and standardized processes streamline IT operations. This leads to faster response times, reduced manual errors, and greater consistency in service delivery.

7. Compliance and Risk Mitigation:

- Infrastructure management ensures that organizations adhere to regulatory and compliance requirements, reducing the risk of legal and financial penalties. It also minimizes operational risks through proactive monitoring.

8. Support for Innovation:

- By freeing IT staff from routine maintenance tasks, infrastructure management enables them to focus on innovation and strategic projects. This agility can lead to the rapid adoption of new technologies.

9. Better User Experience:

- A well-managed infrastructure translates into faster application response times, seamless access to services, and minimal disruptions for both employees and customers.

10. Data-Driven Decision-Making: - Effective infrastructure management enables organizations to collect and analyze data more efficiently. Data-driven insights support informed decision-making and help identify opportunities for improvement.

Challenges of IT Infrastructure Management

While IT Infrastructure Management offers substantial benefits, it also comes with its fair share of challenges. Recognizing and addressing these challenges is essential to ensure a successful management strategy:

1. Complexity:

- Modern IT infrastructures are complex ecosystems with numerous interconnected components. Managing this complexity can be challenging, particularly in hybrid and multi-cloud environments.

2. Rapid Technological Changes:

- The pace of technological change is relentless. Staying up-to-date with new technologies and trends requires continuous learning and adaptation.

3. Security Risks:

- Cybersecurity threats are ever-evolving. IT infrastructure managers must stay vigilant and proactive to protect against data breaches, ransomware, and other threats.

4. Budget Constraints:

- Balancing the need for state-of-the-art infrastructure with budget constraints can be challenging. IT managers often need to make tough decisions to allocate resources effectively.

5. Compliance Requirements:

- Meeting regulatory compliance standards, such as GDPR or HIPAA, can be complex and resource-intensive, adding to the workload of IT infrastructure teams.

6. Talent Shortages:

- Skilled IT infrastructure professionals are in high demand. Organizations may struggle to find and retain talent with the necessary expertise.

7. Legacy Systems:

- Legacy systems can be challenging to integrate with modern infrastructure. Legacy technology may require special attention and resources for maintenance and upgrades.

8. Scalability Issues:

- Scaling infrastructure can be complex, and scaling too rapidly or inefficiently can lead to unexpected challenges and increased costs.

9. Vendor Lock-In:

- Organizations that heavily rely on specific vendors or cloud providers may face challenges in terms of vendor lock-in and limited flexibility.

10. Resistance to Change: - Employees may resist changes in infrastructure management processes or tools, making it challenging to implement new strategies or technologies effectively.

In conclusion, IT Infrastructure Management offers substantial advantages for organizations, including improved reliability, security, cost efficiency, and agility. However, it also presents challenges related to complexity, security risks, budget constraints, and talent shortages. Addressing these challenges and leveraging the benefits is crucial for organizations seeking to maintain a competitive edge in the digital era.

E. Setting Objectives for Effective Infrastructure Management

Setting clear objectives is a fundamental step in ensuring effective infrastructure management within an organization. Objectives provide a roadmap for aligning IT infrastructure with the organization's broader goals, optimizing resource allocation, enhancing efficiency, and achieving measurable results. In this in-depth discussion, we'll explore the process of setting objectives for effective infrastructure management and the key considerations involved.

1. Align with Business Goals:

- The foremost objective of infrastructure management should be to align IT resources with the strategic goals of the organization. Understand the specific business objectives, such as expanding market share, improving customer service, or reducing operational costs, and determine how IT infrastructure can support these goals.

2. Ensure Reliability and Availability:

- High availability and reliability are foundational objectives. Infrastructure should be designed and managed to ensure that critical systems and services are consistently available and perform reliably, minimizing downtime and disruptions.

3. Optimize Resource Utilization:

- Efficiency is a central objective. Ensure that infrastructure resources, including servers, storage, and network bandwidth, are optimally utilized. Over-provisioning and underutilization can lead to unnecessary costs.

4. Enhance Security and Compliance:

- Security and compliance should be top priorities. Objectives in this area may include regular security assessments, vulnerability remediation, and compliance with industry and regulatory standards.

5. Foster Scalability and Flexibility:

- Scalability and flexibility objectives ensure that the infrastructure can adapt to changing business needs. Infrastructure should be able to scale up or down rapidly, accommodating growth or fluctuations in demand.

6. Control Costs and Budget Effectively:

- Cost control objectives involve creating and adhering to IT budgets, minimizing operational expenses, and identifying opportunities for cost optimization, such as consolidation or cloud resource management.

7. Streamline Operations and Automation:

- Streamlining operations through automation is an important objective. Implement Infrastructure as Code (IaC) and automation tools to reduce manual tasks, accelerate provisioning, and improve consistency.

8. Support Innovation and Agility:

- Encourage innovation by setting objectives that allow IT teams to experiment with new technologies and solutions. Agile infrastructure practices enable rapid adoption of emerging technologies.

9. Ensure Disaster Recovery and Business Continuity:

- Disaster recovery and business continuity objectives are critical for minimizing the impact of unforeseen events. Infrastructure management should include robust backup and recovery plans to ensure data and service availability in times of crisis.

10. Enhance User Experience: - User experience objectives aim to deliver seamless access to applications and services, reduce latency, and improve response times, contributing to overall user satisfaction.

11. Implement Monitoring and Analytics: - Monitoring and analytics objectives involve setting up robust monitoring systems to proactively detect and address issues. Analytics can provide insights into infrastructure performance and help make informed decisions.

12. Foster Sustainability: - Sustainability objectives address environmental concerns. Infrastructure management should aim to reduce energy consumption, minimize waste, and promote sustainable practices in data centers and IT operations.

13. Ensure Compliance with Standards: - Ensure that the infrastructure adheres to industry standards and best practices. Compliance objectives may involve regular audits and adherence to security frameworks like ISO 27001 or NIST.

14. Continuously Improve and Evolve: - Infrastructure management should prioritize continuous improvement and evolution. Establish objectives that encourage ongoing assessment, feedback, and adjustment of processes and technologies.

15. Build a Skilled Team: - Investing in human resources is essential. Develop objectives related to team training, skill development, and talent retention to ensure a competent and adaptable infrastructure management team.

16. Foster Collaboration and Communication: - Encourage cross-functional collaboration and clear communication between IT and other business units. Infrastructure management objectives should promote a culture of collaboration.

17. Ensure Vendor Relationships: - For organizations relying on external vendors or cloud providers, objectives related to vendor relationships should ensure service level agreements (SLAs) are met, costs are controlled, and vendor lock-in risks are minimized.

18. Measure and Report Progress: - Finally, establish objectives for measuring and reporting on infrastructure management performance. Key performance indicators (KPIs) should be defined to track progress toward meeting objectives.

In conclusion, setting objectives for effective infrastructure management is a strategic process that should align IT operations with broader organizational goals. These objectives guide decision-making, resource allocation, and continuous improvement efforts. Regularly reviewing and adjusting objectives in response to changing business needs and technological advancements ensures that infrastructure management remains adaptable and aligned with the organization's success.

CHAPTER 2

Introduction to IT Infrastructure Components

In the intricate world of information technology (IT), the term "IT infrastructure components" encompasses the building blocks upon which digital landscapes are constructed. These components are the vital organs of an organization's technological ecosystem, providing the critical functionality that allows data to flow, services to be delivered, and operations to thrive. To embark on a comprehensive exploration of IT infrastructure components, it is essential to understand their fundamental role in modern organizations and how they contribute to the seamless functioning of our digital world. In the following discussion, we will delve into the core components that constitute the intricate tapestry of IT infrastructure, uncovering their significance and interplay in the ever-evolving landscape of technology.

A. Data Centers and Their Role in Infrastructure

Data centers are the nerve centers of modern IT infrastructure, playing a pivotal role in supporting the digital operations of organizations across the globe. These highly specialized facilities are designed to house, process, store, and manage vast amounts of data and computational resources. In this comprehensive exploration, we will delve into the significance of data centers, their key components, and their indispensable role in the infrastructure of today's digital age.

1. The Significance of Data Centers:

- Data centers are the backbone of the digital world. They serve as the centralized repositories for the massive volumes of data generated and utilized by organizations, ranging from financial institutions and healthcare providers to e-commerce platforms and social media giants.

- These facilities ensure data availability, reliability, and security, making them critical for business continuity, disaster recovery, and compliance with regulatory standards.

- Data centers enable the delivery of services and applications, support cloud computing, and facilitate the growing demand for real-time analytics and processing of big data.

2. Key Components of Data Centers:

- **Servers:** Servers form the core computing infrastructure within data centers, executing applications and handling data processing tasks. They come in various forms, including rack-mounted servers, blade servers, and specialized high-performance servers.

- **Storage Systems:** Storage arrays and network-attached storage (NAS) devices store data, ensuring redundancy, scalability, and rapid retrieval of information. These systems are vital for data integrity and resilience.

- **Networking Equipment:** Data centers employ advanced networking components, such as routers, switches, and load balancers, to facilitate seamless communication and data transfer between servers and external networks.

- **Cooling and Power Infrastructure:** Data centers require robust cooling and power systems to maintain a controlled environment and ensure the continuous operation of equipment. This includes precision air conditioning units and uninterruptible power supplies (UPS).

- **Security Measures:** Security is paramount, with data centers implementing physical and digital security measures, including biometric access controls, surveillance systems, and fire suppression systems.

- **Redundancy and High Availability:** Data centers are designed for high availability, featuring redundancy in critical components to minimize downtime. This includes redundant power supplies, network connections, and backup systems.

3. **Role in Business Continuity:**

- Data centers are integral to business continuity strategies. They enable data backup and recovery, ensuring that critical data is preserved and accessible even in the event of hardware failures, natural disasters, or cyberattacks.

- Through redundancy and failover mechanisms, data centers contribute to the seamless delivery of services, reducing the risk of service interruptions that could harm a business's reputation and financial stability.

4. **Support for Cloud Computing:**

- Cloud service providers rely on data centers as the infrastructure underpinning their services. These data centers host virtualized resources, allowing customers to access scalable computing power and storage on-demand.

- Cloud computing, with its flexibility and agility, has revolutionized the way organizations use and manage IT resources, making data centers even more critical in the era of cloud-native technologies.

5. **Scalability and Efficiency:**

- Data centers are designed to be scalable, accommodating the growing demands for processing power and storage capacity. Organizations can add or remove resources as needed, optimizing cost efficiency and resource allocation.

- Virtualization and server consolidation within data centers further enhance efficiency by maximizing resource utilization and reducing the physical footprint.

6. Energy Efficiency and Sustainability:

- As concerns about energy consumption and environmental impact grow, data centers are striving to become more energy-efficient and environmentally sustainable. Techniques such as hot/cold aisle containment, server virtualization, and renewable energy sources contribute to these efforts.

7. Emerging Technologies:

- Data centers are at the forefront of adopting emerging technologies, including artificial intelligence (AI), machine learning, and edge computing. These technologies enhance data processing capabilities, enabling real-time analytics and insights.

In conclusion, data centers are the cornerstone of modern IT infrastructure, facilitating the storage, processing, and management of data critical to businesses and society as a whole. Their role in supporting digital operations, ensuring business continuity, and enabling innovation underscores their significance in an increasingly data-driven world. As technology continues to evolve, data centers will remain at the forefront of technological advancements, shaping the future of IT infrastructure.

B. Hardware Infrastructure (Servers, Networking, Storage)

Hardware infrastructure forms the physical foundation of IT systems, providing the essential computational, networking, and storage resources required for the functioning of modern organizations. This in-depth exploration will delve into the key components of hardware infrastructure—servers, networking equipment, and storage systems—examining their roles, types, and significance within the broader landscape of IT infrastructure.

1. Servers:

- **Role:** Servers are the workhorses of IT infrastructure, responsible for processing and serving applications, data, and services to end-users and client devices. They respond to requests, execute software, and manage data.

- **Types of Servers:**

  - **Application Servers:** Host and execute application software, delivering services to users. Examples include web servers and database servers.

  - **File Servers:** Store and manage files, enabling users to share and access data within an organization.

- **Mail Servers:** Manage email communications, handling incoming and outgoing messages.

- **Virtualization Servers:** Host virtual machines (VMs) through hypervisors, allowing for efficient resource utilization and management.

- **Scalability:** Servers can be scaled horizontally (adding more servers) or vertically (upgrading existing servers) to meet changing performance and capacity requirements.

2. Networking Equipment:

- **Role:** Networking equipment facilitates communication and data transfer between devices and across networks. It ensures that data packets are routed accurately to their destinations.

- **Types of Networking Equipment:**

    - **Routers:** Connect different networks, directing data traffic between them.

    - **Switches:** Connect devices within a network, enabling data transmission between devices.

    - **Firewalls:** Protect networks by monitoring and filtering incoming and outgoing traffic to block potential threats.

- **Load Balancers:** Distribute incoming network traffic across multiple servers, ensuring even load distribution and high availability.

- **Access Points:** Provide wireless connectivity to devices, allowing them to connect to a network without physical cables.

- **Scalability:** Networking equipment can be scaled to accommodate increased network traffic and device connectivity.

3. Storage Systems:

- **Role:** Storage systems provide the means to store, retrieve, and manage data. They ensure data availability, reliability, and durability.

- **Types of Storage Systems:**

  - **Direct-Attached Storage (DAS):** Storage devices directly connected to a single server or host.

  - **Network-Attached Storage (NAS):** Specialized storage devices accessed over a network, often used for file sharing.

  - **Storage Area Network (SAN):** High-performance network dedicated to connecting storage devices and servers, commonly used for block-level storage.

- **Object Storage:** Stores data as objects with associated metadata, suitable for scalable and distributed storage needs.

- **Redundancy:** Redundant storage configurations, such as RAID (Redundant Array of Independent Disks), are employed to protect against data loss and ensure data integrity.

- **Scalability:** Storage systems can be scaled by adding more drives, expanding storage arrays, or adopting cloud storage solutions to accommodate data growth.

4. Significance of Hardware Infrastructure:

- **Performance:** Hardware infrastructure directly impacts system performance, influencing the speed and responsiveness of applications and services.

- **Reliability:** High-quality hardware is crucial for ensuring system uptime and data integrity, reducing the risk of hardware failures and associated downtime.

- **Scalability:** Scalable hardware infrastructure allows organizations to adapt to changing workloads and business requirements without significant disruptions.

- **Security:** Hardware components can contribute to overall system security through features like hardware-based encryption and secure boot processes.

- **Cost Efficiency:** Efficient hardware utilization, through technologies like virtualization and consolidation, can lead to cost savings and better resource allocation.

In conclusion, hardware infrastructure comprising servers, networking equipment, and storage systems serves as the fundamental building blocks of modern IT environments. Their proper selection, configuration, and management are critical for ensuring optimal performance, scalability, reliability, and security. As organizations continue to rely on technology for their operations, the role of hardware infrastructure in supporting business objectives remains indispensable, making it a cornerstone of IT infrastructure management.

C. Software Infrastructure (Operating Systems, Virtualization)

Software infrastructure is the invisible but essential counterpart to hardware infrastructure in modern IT ecosystems. It comprises the foundational software components that enable the management, orchestration, and execution of applications, services, and data. In this comprehensive exploration, we will delve into two key elements of software infrastructure: operating systems and virtualization technologies, examining their roles, types, and significance within the broader landscape of IT infrastructure.

1. Operating Systems:

- **Role:** Operating systems (OS) are the core software that manages hardware resources and provides essential services to support the execution of applications and software. They act as intermediaries between hardware and software, abstracting hardware complexity.

- **Types of Operating Systems:**

  - **Server Operating Systems:** Optimized for server environments, these OS versions prioritize stability, security, and scalability. Examples include Windows Server, Linux Server distributions (e.g., CentOS, Ubuntu Server), and Unix variants.

  - **Desktop Operating Systems:** Designed for personal computers and workstations, desktop OS versions emphasize user-friendliness, productivity, and application compatibility. Examples include Windows, macOS, and various Linux desktop distributions.

  - **Mobile Operating Systems:** Engineered for smartphones and tablets, mobile OS versions focus on touch interfaces, portability, and app ecosystems. Examples include Android, iOS, and HarmonyOS.

- **Embedded Operating Systems:** Deployed in embedded systems like IoT devices, industrial equipment, and appliances, these OS versions prioritize minimal resource usage and real-time capabilities. Examples include FreeRTOS, VxWorks, and Embedded Linux.

- **Functionality:** Operating systems provide core functionalities such as process management, memory management, file system management, device driver support, and user interface components.

- **Security:** Security features, such as user authentication, access control, and firewall configurations, are integrated into operating systems to protect against threats and vulnerabilities.

- **Virtualization Support:** Many modern OS versions include features to support virtualization, enabling the creation and management of virtual machines (VMs) and containers.

2. Virtualization Technologies:

- **Role:** Virtualization technologies create virtualized instances of hardware resources, allowing multiple operating systems and applications to run independently on a single physical server or host.

- **Types of Virtualization Technologies:**

    - **Server Virtualization:** Hypervisors, like VMware vSphere, Microsoft Hyper-V, and KVM, enable the creation of VMs, each running its own OS and applications on a shared physical server.

    - **Desktop Virtualization:** Technologies such as VMware Horizon and Citrix Virtual Apps and Desktops deliver virtualized desktop environments to end-users, enabling secure access from various devices.

    - **Application Virtualization:** This approach, exemplified by Docker and Kubernetes, packages applications and their dependencies into containers, ensuring consistent execution across different environments.

    - **Network Virtualization:** Technologies like SDN (Software-Defined Networking) and NFV (Network Functions Virtualization) virtualize network resources, enhancing network flexibility and manageability.

- **Benefits:** Virtualization brings several advantages, including improved resource utilization, scalability, agility, reduced hardware costs, disaster recovery capabilities, and simplified management.

- **Containerization:** Containerization, a form of virtualization, has gained popularity for its lightweight and efficient approach to packaging and deploying applications in isolated environments. Docker and Kubernetes are leading containerization technologies.

3. Significance of Software Infrastructure:

- **Abstraction and Portability:** Software infrastructure abstracts underlying hardware complexity, enhancing portability and enabling applications to run across diverse hardware platforms.

- **Resource Optimization:** Virtualization technologies optimize resource utilization, allowing organizations to maximize their IT investments by consolidating workloads and reducing hardware requirements.

- **Scalability:** Software infrastructure supports the dynamic allocation and scaling of resources, ensuring systems can adapt to changing workloads and demands.

- **Security and Isolation:** Virtualization and containerization technologies enhance security by isolating workloads from each other, preventing conflicts and potential security breaches.

- **Management and Automation:** Software infrastructure facilitates centralized management and automation of IT resources, streamlining administrative tasks and reducing operational overhead.

In conclusion, software infrastructure, comprising operating systems and virtualization technologies, serves as the invisible but indispensable foundation of modern IT ecosystems. These software components play pivotal roles in abstracting hardware complexity, optimizing resource utilization, enhancing security, and enabling portability and scalability. As organizations continue to rely on technology to achieve their goals, the role of software infrastructure in orchestrating and managing IT resources remains central to the efficient functioning of IT environments.

D. Network Architecture (LAN, WAN, VPN)

Network architecture is the blueprint that defines the structure, protocols, and components of a computer network. It encompasses the design and layout of networks that connect devices, systems, and users to facilitate communication and data exchange. In this comprehensive exploration, we will delve into the key aspects of network architecture, including Local Area Networks (LANs), Wide Area Networks (WANs), and Virtual Private Networks

(VPNs), examining their roles, types, and significance within the broader landscape of IT infrastructure.

1. Local Area Networks (LANs):

- **Role:** LANs are localized networks that connect devices within a limited geographic area, typically within a single building or campus. They provide fast, high-bandwidth connectivity for devices such as computers, printers, and servers.

- **Components:** LANs include devices like switches and routers to manage data traffic, Ethernet cables or wireless access points for connectivity, and network protocols (e.g., TCP/IP) for communication.

- **Topologies:** Common LAN topologies include star, bus, and ring configurations, with Ethernet being the most widely used LAN technology.

- **Significance:** LANs enable seamless communication, file sharing, and resource access within organizations, fostering collaboration and productivity among local users.

2. Wide Area Networks (WANs):

- **Role:** WANs connect geographically dispersed LANs, extending network connectivity over a broader area, often across cities, regions, or even continents. They facilitate data exchange between distant locations.

- **Components:** WANs utilize various technologies, including routers, leased lines, optical fiber, and satellite links. They also rely on WAN protocols such as MPLS (Multi-Protocol Label Switching) and BGP (Border Gateway Protocol).

- **Topologies:** WANs can have different topologies, but the most common is the hub-and-spoke model, where a central location (hub) connects to multiple remote sites (spokes).

- **Significance:** WANs enable organizations to connect remote offices, branches, and data centers, supporting centralized data storage, distributed applications, and global communication.

3. Virtual Private Networks (VPNs):

- **Role:** VPNs create secure, encrypted communication channels over public or untrusted networks, such as the internet. They enable remote users or branch offices to access private networks securely.

- **Types of VPNs:**

  - **Site-to-Site VPNs:** Connect multiple LANs across different locations, extending secure network connectivity.

  - **Remote Access VPNs:** Enable individual users or

remote devices to connect securely to a corporate network, often using VPN clients.

- **SSL VPNs:** Provide secure access to web-based applications and services, typically through a web browser.

- **Security:** VPNs use encryption protocols like IPsec (Internet Protocol Security) or SSL/TLS (Secure Sockets Layer/Transport Layer Security) to ensure data confidentiality and integrity.

- **Significance:** VPNs enhance security by protecting data during transmission over public networks, making them essential for remote work, telecommuting, and secure access to cloud services.

4. Significance of Network Architecture:

- **Connectivity:** Network architecture facilitates seamless communication and data exchange between devices and systems, enabling organizations to operate efficiently and share resources.

- **Scalability:** Scalable network architecture supports the growth of an organization, allowing for the addition of new devices and locations as needed.

- **Reliability:** Redundancy and failover mechanisms in network architecture ensure high availability and minimize downtime.

- **Security:** Network architecture incorporates security measures, such as firewalls, intrusion detection systems (IDS), and access controls, to protect against unauthorized access and cyber threats.

- **Remote Access:** VPNs and WANs enable remote access to resources, supporting remote work, branch office connectivity, and global collaboration.

In conclusion, network architecture is a fundamental element of IT infrastructure, serving as the foundation for communication, connectivity, and data exchange within organizations. LANs, WANs, and VPNs are integral components that ensure local and global connectivity while providing security and scalability. As businesses continue to expand and adapt to changing technological landscapes, the design and management of network architecture remain critical for achieving organizational goals and maintaining a competitive edge.

E. Emerging Technologies in Infrastructure

The field of IT infrastructure is constantly evolving, driven by innovations and emerging technologies that shape the way organizations build, manage, and optimize their digital ecosystems. In this in-depth exploration, we will delve into some of the most impactful emerging technologies in infrastructure, their significance, and how they are reshaping the landscape of IT infrastructure management.

1. **Edge Computing:**

- **Significance:** Edge computing brings computational resources closer to the data source or end-users, reducing latency and enabling real-time data processing. This is particularly crucial for applications like IoT devices, autonomous vehicles, and augmented reality (AR) that require low-latency responses.

- **Use Cases:** Edge computing finds applications in industries such as manufacturing, healthcare, and smart cities, where processing data at the edge allows for faster decision-making and improved operational efficiency.

- **Technologies:** Edge devices, edge servers, and edge analytics platforms are key components that enable edge computing.

2. **5G Networking:**

- **Significance:** The fifth generation of wireless networking, 5G, offers significantly higher data rates, lower latency, and improved reliability compared to its predecessors. It is poised to revolutionize connectivity across various industries.

- **Use Cases:** 5G enables high-bandwidth applications like augmented reality, virtual reality, autonomous vehicles, and remote surgery. It also facilitates IoT deployments at a massive scale.

- **Impact on Infrastructure:** 5G infrastructure includes small cell networks, millimeter-wave technology, and software-defined networking (SDN) to deliver the required performance.

3. AI and Machine Learning:

- **Significance:** AI and machine learning are transforming infrastructure management by automating tasks, predicting system failures, and optimizing resource allocation. They enhance efficiency, security, and decision-making.

- **Use Cases:** AI-driven analytics improve network performance, security, and troubleshooting. In data centers, machine learning optimizes server utilization, energy efficiency, and predictive maintenance.

- **Technologies:** AI-powered monitoring tools, anomaly detection, and predictive analytics platforms are instrumental in implementing AI and machine learning in infrastructure management.

4. Containers and Kubernetes:

- **Significance:** Containers and container orchestration tools like Kubernetes have revolutionized application deployment and management. They enable the packaging of applications and their dependencies for consistent deployment across diverse environments.

- **Use Cases:** Containers simplify the deployment of microservices, DevOps practices, and cloud-native applications. They offer portability and scalability advantages.

- **Impact on Infrastructure:** Infrastructure as Code (IaC) and container orchestration platforms automate infrastructure provisioning, scaling, and management.

5. Hybrid and Multi-Cloud Environments:

- **Significance:** Organizations are increasingly adopting hybrid and multi-cloud strategies to leverage the flexibility and scalability of public clouds while maintaining control over sensitive data and critical workloads.

- **Use Cases:** Hybrid and multi-cloud environments allow organizations to balance cost, performance, and compliance requirements by distributing workloads across on-premises data centers and multiple cloud providers.

- **Impact on Infrastructure:** Infrastructure management tools and practices must evolve to support the seamless integration and orchestration of resources across multiple cloud platforms.

6. Blockchain Technology:

- **Significance:** Blockchain is a distributed ledger technology that offers transparency, security, and immutability. It has applications in supply chain management, secure transactions, and digital identity.

- **Use Cases:** Blockchain can be used for secure data sharing, authentication, and tracking in various industries, including finance, healthcare, and logistics.

- **Impact on Infrastructure:** Implementing blockchain requires the deployment of nodes and consensus mechanisms, which can impact infrastructure design and resource allocation.

7. Quantum Computing:

- **Significance:** Quantum computing promises unprecedented computational power, potentially solving complex problems that are currently infeasible for classical computers.

- **Use Cases:** Quantum computing can impact fields like cryptography, materials science, optimization, and drug discovery, among others.

- **Infrastructure Challenges:** Quantum computers require

specialized infrastructure due to their extreme sensitivity to environmental factors like temperature and electromagnetic interference.

In conclusion, emerging technologies in infrastructure are reshaping the way organizations build, manage, and optimize their digital ecosystems. Edge computing, 5G networking, AI and machine learning, containers, hybrid and multi-cloud environments, blockchain, and quantum computing are driving innovation and enabling organizations to stay competitive in an increasingly digital and interconnected world. Staying abreast of these emerging technologies and their potential applications is crucial for IT infrastructure professionals and organizations aiming to harness their benefits.

CHAPTER 3

IT Infrastructure Planning and Design

In the ever-evolving landscape of information technology, the planning and design of IT infrastructure stand as fundamental pillars upon which the reliability, scalability, and efficiency of an organization's digital ecosystem are built. IT infrastructure planning and design involve the meticulous orchestration of resources, technologies, and strategies to ensure that the technological backbone of an organization aligns seamlessly with its objectives and requirements. In the following discussion, we embark on a journey through the realm of IT infrastructure planning and design, exploring the critical considerations, methodologies, and significance that underpin the creation of resilient and future-ready digital environments.

A. Capacity Planning in IT Infrastructure

Capacity planning is a critical aspect of IT infrastructure management that involves strategically forecasting and allocating computing resources to meet current and future demands efficiently. It is a multifaceted process that requires a deep understanding of an organization's current infrastructure, its growth trajectory, and the evolving technology landscape. In this in-depth exploration, we will delve into the significance of capacity planning, its key components, methodologies, and its crucial role in ensuring the optimal performance and scalability of IT systems.

1. **Significance of Capacity Planning:**

- **Optimal Resource Utilization:** Capacity planning ensures that IT resources, including processing power, memory, storage, and network bandwidth, are used efficiently. It helps avoid over-provisioning, which can lead to wasted resources, and under-provisioning, which can result in performance bottlenecks.

- **Cost Control:** By accurately predicting resource needs, organizations can manage IT costs effectively. Overinvesting in unnecessary infrastructure or grappling with sudden resource shortages can be costly.

- **Performance Assurance:** Capacity planning helps maintain consistent system performance, ensuring that applications and services meet user expectations. It minimizes the risk of slow response times and downtime.

- **Scalability:** A well-executed capacity plan provides a roadmap for scaling IT resources in response to business growth, seasonal fluctuations, or increased workloads.

2. Components of Capacity Planning:

- **Performance Monitoring:** Continuously monitor the performance of IT systems, collecting data on resource utilization, response times, and transaction volumes.

- **Demand Forecasting:** Analyze historical usage patterns and future business projections to estimate resource demands accurately.

- **Resource Modeling:** Create models that represent the relationships between different resources and their impact on system performance. This helps in predicting the effects of resource changes.

- **Scenario Planning:** Develop scenarios that anticipate various growth and usage scenarios, allowing for proactive resource allocation.

- **Benchmarking:** Compare current system performance against industry standards and best practices to identify areas for improvement.

- **Capacity Testing:** Conduct load testing and stress testing to validate the capacity plan's effectiveness and identify potential bottlenecks.

3. Capacity Planning Methodologies:

- **Analytical Modeling:** This method involves using mathematical models to predict system behavior under different conditions. It is especially useful for predicting performance in complex, dynamic environments.

- **Workload Characterization:** Analyzing the types of workloads that the infrastructure will encounter allows for more accurate capacity planning. This method often involves classifying workloads by their resource requirements and usage patterns.

- **Trend Analysis:** Historical performance data is analyzed to identify trends and extrapolate future resource needs. Statistical methods and forecasting techniques are often employed.

- **Resource Allocation Policies:** Implement policies for resource allocation based on business priorities. This can involve setting resource allocation rules, such as prioritizing critical applications.

- **Cloud Scaling:** For organizations utilizing cloud services, capacity planning involves understanding the scaling options provided by cloud providers and optimizing resource usage in the cloud environment.

4. Challenges in Capacity Planning:

- **Data Accuracy:** Capacity planning relies on accurate data, and collecting such data can be challenging. Inaccurate data can lead to flawed predictions.

- **Complexity:** Modern IT environments are complex, with diverse systems and interdependencies. Capturing all relevant factors for capacity planning can be daunting.

- **Changing Workloads:** Dynamic workloads, influenced by factors like seasonality or sudden spikes in demand, can make capacity planning more challenging.

- **Technological Advancements:** Rapid advancements in technology introduce new variables and opportunities that capacity planners must account for.

- **Cost Constraints:** Balancing resource allocation with budget limitations is a constant challenge in capacity planning.

In conclusion, capacity planning is an integral aspect of IT infrastructure management that bridges the gap between an organization's technology resources and its operational needs. When executed effectively, it ensures that IT systems operate optimally, efficiently, and cost-effectively, even in the face of changing demands and technology trends. Capacity planning is not a one-time endeavor but an ongoing process that adapts to the evolving needs of the organization, helping it stay agile, competitive, and prepared for future growth.

B. Scalability and Redundancy in IT Infrastructure

Scalability and redundancy are two core principles in IT infrastructure design and management. They are essential for ensuring that an organization's digital systems can accommodate growth, handle increasing workloads, and maintain high availability and reliability. In this in-depth exploration, we will delve into the significance of scalability and redundancy, their key components, methodologies, and their crucial roles in building robust and flexible IT environments.

1. Scalability:

1.1 Significance:

- **Adapting to Growth:** Scalability is the ability of an IT infrastructure to handle increasing workloads and resource demands without compromising performance or reliability. It ensures that as an organization grows, its digital systems can scale to meet new demands.

- **Optimal Resource Utilization:** Scalable systems are designed to allocate resources dynamically, ensuring that computing power, storage, and network bandwidth are used efficiently. This helps in cost control and resource optimization.

- **Business Agility:** Scalability supports business agility by allowing organizations to respond quickly to changing market conditions, customer demands, and competitive pressures.

1.2 Components of Scalability:

- **Horizontal Scalability:** Also known as "scaling out," this approach involves adding more identical components, such as servers or nodes, to the infrastructure. It is commonly used in distributed systems and cloud computing.

- **Vertical Scalability:** Also known as "scaling up," this approach involves increasing the capacity of individual components, typically by upgrading hardware resources. It is often used in traditional data center environments.

- **Elasticity:** Elasticity is the ability to automatically and dynamically adjust resource allocation based on demand. It is a key feature of cloud computing environments.

- **Load Balancing:** Load balancers distribute incoming traffic across multiple servers or resources, ensuring even resource utilization and preventing overloading of any single component.

1.3 Scalability Methodologies:

- **Capacity Planning:** Predicting future resource requirements based on historical data and business projections to ensure that additional resources are provisioned in advance.

- **Auto-Scaling:** Implementing automated scaling policies that add or remove resources in response to changing workloads. This is commonly used in cloud environments.

- **Containerization and Orchestration:** Technologies like Docker and Kubernetes enable the efficient deployment and scaling of containerized applications.

- **Microservices Architecture:** Breaking down monolithic applications into smaller, independently deployable services allows for granular scalability.

2. Redundancy:

2.1 Significance:

- **High Availability:** Redundancy is the practice of duplicating critical components or systems to ensure that if one fails, another takes over seamlessly. It is essential for achieving high availability and minimizing downtime.

- **Fault Tolerance:** Redundancy enhances fault tolerance by providing backup systems that can continue operations in case of hardware failures, software crashes, or other unexpected events.

- **Data Integrity:** Redundant storage and backup solutions protect data from loss or corruption, ensuring data integrity and compliance with data protection regulations.

2.2 Components of Redundancy:

- **Hardware Redundancy:** This includes duplicating hardware components such as servers, power supplies, and network switches. In the event of a hardware failure, the redundant component takes over.

- **Network Redundancy:** Redundant network paths and connections ensure that data can flow even if one network route becomes unavailable. Technologies like Spanning Tree Protocol (STP) manage network redundancy.

- **Data Redundancy:** Redundant storage systems, such as RAID arrays, replicate data across multiple disks to protect against data loss. Backup and disaster recovery solutions also provide data redundancy.

- **Load Balancer Redundancy:** Load balancers themselves can be made redundant to ensure uninterrupted traffic distribution.

2.3 Redundancy Methodologies:

- **Active-Passive Redundancy:** One component (active) handles the workload while the redundant component (passive) remains inactive until needed. Failover occurs when the active component fails.

- **Active-Active Redundancy:** Both redundant components are active and share the workload. This approach is more efficient but requires careful load balancing.

- **Geographic Redundancy:** Duplicating infrastructure in different geographic locations to protect against regional disasters, such as earthquakes or floods.

3. Balancing Scalability and Redundancy:

- Achieving the right balance between scalability and redundancy is essential. Over-emphasizing one can lead to resource underutilization or excessive complexity.

- Careful planning, capacity modeling, and risk assessment help determine the appropriate levels of scalability and redundancy for an organization's specific needs.

- Cloud computing platforms often provide scalable and redundant infrastructure services, allowing organizations to focus on their applications and services rather than infrastructure management.

In conclusion, scalability and redundancy are fundamental principles in IT infrastructure design, ensuring that digital systems can grow to meet evolving demands and maintain high availability and reliability. Effective implementation of these principles requires a deep understanding of an organization's requirements, careful planning, and the selection of appropriate technologies and methodologies. Balancing these two principles is key to building resilient and adaptable IT environments that can support an organization's current and future needs.

C. Disaster Recovery and Business Continuity in IT Infrastructure

Disaster recovery (DR) and business continuity (BC) are critical aspects of IT infrastructure management, aimed at ensuring an organization's ability to recover from unexpected disruptions and maintain essential operations. These disruptions can range from natural disasters to cyberattacks and system failures. In this in-depth exploration, we will delve into the significance of disaster recovery and business continuity, their key components, methodologies, and their crucial roles in safeguarding an organization's data, services, and resilience.

1. Significance of Disaster Recovery and Business Continuity:

1.1. Disaster Recovery (DR):

- **Minimizing Downtime:** DR planning focuses on minimizing downtime and data loss in the event of a disaster, system failure, or other disruptive events. This ensures that an organization can continue its operations as quickly as possible.

- **Data Protection:** DR encompasses data backup, replication, and recovery strategies that protect critical data and prevent data loss, which is vital for regulatory compliance and business integrity.

- **Reputation Management:** Effective disaster recovery measures help maintain an organization's reputation by demonstrating its commitment to business resilience and customer service.

1.2. Business Continuity (BC):

- **Preserving Core Functions:** BC planning ensures that essential business functions can continue despite disruptions. It encompasses not only IT but also people, processes, and facilities.

- **Risk Mitigation:** BC planning identifies potential risks and vulnerabilities, allowing organizations to implement risk mitigation strategies and reduce the impact of disruptive events.

- **Regulatory Compliance:** Many industries and regions require organizations to have BC plans in place to meet regulatory compliance standards.

2. Components of Disaster Recovery and Business Continuity:

2.1. Disaster Recovery:

- **Data Backup and Recovery:** Regularly back up critical data and establish procedures for swift data recovery, including full and incremental backups.

- **Redundant Systems:** Implement redundant systems and infrastructure to ensure service availability and minimize downtime.

- **Failover and Replication:** Configure failover mechanisms and data replication to maintain service continuity in the event of system failures.

- **Disaster Recovery Sites:** Establish secondary data centers or cloud-based disaster recovery sites for data and application recovery.

- **Testing and Simulation:** Regularly test DR plans through drills and simulations to identify weaknesses and improve recovery procedures.

2.2. Business Continuity:

- **Business Impact Analysis (BIA):** Conduct a BIA to identify critical business processes, dependencies, and the potential impact of disruptions.

- **Risk Assessment:** Assess risks and vulnerabilities to identify potential disruptive events, such as natural disasters, cybersecurity threats, or supply chain disruptions.

- **Crisis Management:** Develop a crisis management team and a communication plan to coordinate responses and actions during a crisis.

- **Workplace Recovery:** Establish alternate work locations, remote work capabilities, and procedures for employees to continue working during disruptions.

- **Supply Chain Resilience:** Ensure that supply chains and vendor relationships are resilient to disruptions and can be quickly adapted to maintain operations.

3. Methodologies and Strategies:

3.1. Disaster Recovery:

- **Recovery Time Objective (RTO):** Define the maximum

acceptable downtime for systems and services, guiding the recovery process.

- **Recovery Point Objective (RPO):** Determine the maximum data loss acceptable in the event of a disaster, guiding data backup and recovery frequency.

- **Cloud-Based Disaster Recovery:** Leveraging cloud services for backup and recovery can provide cost-effective and scalable DR solutions.

- **Replication Technologies:** Employ data replication technologies like synchronous and asynchronous replication to ensure data consistency.

3.2. Business Continuity:

- **Business Continuity Planning (BCP):** Develop comprehensive BCPs that encompass all aspects of the organization, including people, processes, technology, and facilities.

- **Incident Response Plans:** Create detailed incident response plans that outline actions to be taken during specific events, including cybersecurity incidents and natural disasters.

- **Supply Chain Risk Management:** Collaborate with suppliers and partners to enhance supply chain resilience and diversify sourcing to mitigate risks.

- **Employee Training and Awareness:** Ensure that employees are trained and aware of their roles and responsibilities during disruptive events.

4. Testing and Maintenance:

- Regularly test DR and BC plans through tabletop exercises, simulations, and live drills to validate their effectiveness.

- Continuously update and maintain DR and BC plans to account for evolving threats, technologies, and organizational changes.

- Document lessons learned from tests and real-world incidents to improve response and recovery procedures.

In conclusion, disaster recovery and business continuity are indispensable elements of IT infrastructure management that protect an organization's operations, data, and reputation in the face of unforeseen disruptions. Effective planning, comprehensive strategies, regular testing, and continuous improvement are essential for ensuring resilience and recovery capabilities that can withstand a wide range of disruptive events. Investing in these measures not only safeguards an organization's future but also demonstrates its commitment to the safety and well-being of its employees, customers, and stakeholders.

D. Security Considerations in IT Infrastructure

Security considerations are paramount in IT infrastructure management. Protecting an organization's digital assets, data, and systems from a diverse range of threats is critical for business continuity, data privacy, and regulatory compliance. In this in-depth exploration, we will delve into the significance of security considerations, key components, methodologies, and their crucial roles in safeguarding IT infrastructure.

1. Significance of Security Considerations:

1.1. Data Protection:

- **Data Privacy:** Security measures protect sensitive data from unauthorized access, ensuring compliance with data protection regulations such as GDPR and HIPAA.

- **Data Integrity:** Security safeguards prevent data tampering and corruption, ensuring the accuracy and reliability of data.

1.2. Business Continuity:

- **Resilience:** Security measures enhance the resilience of IT infrastructure by safeguarding against cyberattacks, system failures, and other disruptive events.

- **Continuity Planning:** Security considerations are essential components of business continuity and disaster recovery planning.

1.3. Reputation Management:

- **Trust:** A strong security posture builds trust with customers, partners, and stakeholders.

- **Reputation Protection:** Effective security measures protect an organization's reputation by preventing data breaches and cyber incidents.

2. Components of Security Considerations:

2.1. Access Control:

- **Authentication:** Verify the identity of users and devices, typically through methods such as passwords, multi-factor authentication (MFA), and biometrics.

- **Authorization:** Define access rights and permissions for users and systems to ensure that only authorized individuals can access specific resources.

2.2. Network Security:

- **Firewalls:** Implement firewalls to filter network traffic and protect against unauthorized access and threats.

- **Intrusion Detection and Prevention Systems (IDPS):** Deploy IDPS to monitor network traffic for suspicious activities and prevent intrusions.

- **Virtual Private Networks (VPNs):** Use VPNs to encrypt network communication and secure remote access.

2.3. Endpoint Security:

- **Antivirus and Anti-Malware:** Install antivirus and anti-malware software on endpoints to detect and remove malicious software.

- **Endpoint Detection and Response (EDR):** EDR solutions monitor and respond to security threats at the endpoint level.

2.4. Data Encryption:

- **Data in Transit:** Encrypt data transmitted over networks to prevent eavesdropping and interception.

- **Data at Rest:** Encrypt data stored on storage devices, including hard drives and databases.

2.5. Vulnerability Management:

- **Patch Management:** Regularly apply security patches and updates to systems and software to address known vulnerabilities.

- **Vulnerability Scanning:** Conduct vulnerability assessments to identify weaknesses in the infrastructure and prioritize remediation.

2.6. Incident Response:

- **Incident Identification:** Establish procedures for promptly detecting and identifying security incidents.

- **Incident Containment:** Develop plans to isolate and contain security breaches to prevent further damage.

- **Incident Recovery:** Define recovery steps and actions to return systems to normal operation after an incident.

2.7. Security Awareness and Training:

- **Employee Training:** Provide security awareness training to employees to educate them on security best practices and the risks associated with cyber threats.

- **Phishing Awareness:** Train employees to recognize and report phishing attempts and other social engineering tactics.

3. Methodologies and Strategies:

3.1. Defense in Depth:

- Implement multiple layers of security measures to create a robust defense against diverse threats. This includes a combination of network security, endpoint security, access control, and more.

3.2. Zero Trust Security:

- Adopt a zero trust security model that assumes that threats may exist both inside and outside the network. Verify the identity and trustworthiness of all users and devices, regardless of their location.

3.3. Security Policies and Compliance:

- Develop and enforce security policies that align with industry standards and regulatory requirements.

- Regularly audit and assess compliance with security policies.

4. Testing and Evaluation:

- Conduct regular security assessments, penetration testing, and vulnerability scans to identify and remediate weaknesses in the infrastructure.

- Continuously monitor for security incidents and anomalous activities.

5. Security Incident Reporting:

- Establish clear procedures for reporting security incidents and breaches to relevant authorities, customers, and stakeholders.

In conclusion, security considerations are integral to IT infrastructure management and are essential for safeguarding an organization's digital assets, ensuring data privacy, and maintaining business continuity. Implementing a comprehensive security strategy, including access control, network and endpoint security, encryption, vulnerability management, and incident response, is vital to mitigating risks and protecting against evolving threats. Security awareness, compliance, and a proactive approach to testing and evaluation are key elements of a robust security posture that enables organizations to navigate the ever-evolving threat landscape with confidence.

E. Cost Estimation and Budgeting in IT Infrastructure

Cost estimation and budgeting play a pivotal role in IT infrastructure management. Accurately forecasting and managing expenses are essential to ensure that an organization's technology investments align with its strategic goals, while also maintaining financial sustainability. In this in-depth exploration, we will delve into the significance of cost estimation and budgeting, key components, methodologies, and their crucial roles in optimizing IT infrastructure investments.

1. Significance of Cost Estimation and Budgeting:

1.1. Financial Planning:

- **Strategic Alignment:** Cost estimation and budgeting help align technology investments with an organization's strategic objectives.

- **Resource Allocation:** They facilitate the allocation of financial resources to IT initiatives, ensuring that critical projects receive adequate funding.

1.2. Cost Control:

- **Expense Tracking:** Accurate budgeting allows for the tracking of actual expenses, enabling organizations to identify cost overruns and take corrective actions.

- **Resource Optimization:** Cost estimation helps optimize resource allocation, ensuring that resources are used efficiently and wastage is minimized.

1.3. Risk Management:

- **Risk Assessment:** Cost estimation considers potential risks and uncertainties, allowing organizations to build contingencies into their budgets.

- **Resource Planning:** Budgeting helps organizations plan for unexpected events or emergencies that may impact IT infrastructure.

2. Components of Cost Estimation and Budgeting:

2.1. Cost Estimation:

- **Hardware and Software Costs:** Estimate the costs of purchasing and licensing hardware and software components required for infrastructure projects.

- **Labor Costs:** Consider personnel costs, including salaries, benefits, and training, for IT staff involved in project implementation.

- **Third-party Services:** Include costs related to outsourcing services, such as cloud computing, managed services, or consulting.

- **Infrastructure Costs:** Account for expenses associated with data center facilities, networking equipment, and other infrastructure components.

- **Contingency Costs:** Allocate a portion of the budget for unexpected expenses or scope changes.

2.2. Budgeting:

- **Capital Expenditure (CapEx):** Allocate funds for capital investments, such as purchasing servers, networking equipment, and infrastructure upgrades.

- **Operating Expenditure (OpEx):** Budget for ongoing operational costs, including salaries, maintenance, licensing fees, and utility expenses.

- **Project Budgets:** Create project-specific budgets for individual IT initiatives, ensuring that they are adequately funded.

- **Cost Allocation:** Allocate costs to specific departments or projects to ensure transparency and accountability.

- **Annual Budgets:** Develop annual budgets that encompass all IT-related expenses and align with the organization's fiscal year.

3. Methodologies and Strategies:

3.1. Bottom-Up Estimation:

- Gather detailed cost estimates from individual project teams or departments to create a comprehensive IT budget.

- Consider the specific requirements and scope of each project to determine accurate cost estimates.

3.2. Top-Down Estimation:

- Start with an overall budget figure determined by senior management or finance.

- Allocate budgetary amounts to various IT projects and initiatives based on strategic priorities.

3.3. Total Cost of Ownership (TCO):

- Calculate the TCO for IT infrastructure investments, which includes not only upfront costs but also ongoing operational expenses over the life of the investment.

- TCO analysis helps in making informed decisions about the long-term financial impact of technology investments.

3.4. Return on Investment (ROI):

- Evaluate the expected ROI for IT projects by comparing the anticipated benefits, such as increased productivity or revenue, to the estimated costs.

- ROI analysis assists in prioritizing projects with the highest potential returns.

3.5. Budget Monitoring and Adjustments:

- Regularly monitor actual expenses against budgeted amounts.

- Make adjustments to the budget as needed based on changing project requirements, unexpected expenses, or shifts in strategic priorities.

4. Cost Optimization:

- Continuously seek opportunities for cost optimization by identifying areas where expenses can be reduced or resources can be better utilized.

- Explore technologies and practices, such as virtualization, cloud computing, and automation, that can lead to cost savings.

5. Risk Management:

- Build risk contingencies into the budget to account for unforeseen events that may impact project costs.

- Regularly assess and update risk assessments to minimize potential financial surprises.

In conclusion, cost estimation and budgeting are integral components of IT infrastructure management that enable organizations to make informed financial decisions, allocate resources efficiently, and align technology investments with strategic objectives. Effective cost estimation involves considering various factors, including hardware, software, labor, and contingency costs. Budgeting encompasses capital and operational expenses, project-specific budgets, and annual financial planning. By implementing robust methodologies, monitoring budgets diligently, and optimizing costs, organizations can achieve fiscal responsibility and maximize the value of their IT infrastructure investments.

CHAPTER 4

IT Service Management (ITSM)

In the modern landscape of information technology, the seamless and efficient delivery of IT services has become the linchpin of organizational success. IT Service Management (ITSM) emerges as the structured and strategic approach that guides organizations in planning, delivering, managing, and continually improving IT services to meet business needs and ensure customer satisfaction. As we embark on this exploration, we delve into the realm of ITSM, uncovering its significance, key principles, methodologies, and the pivotal role it plays in harmonizing technology with the ever-evolving demands of businesses and their stakeholders.

A. ITIL Framework and Best Practices in IT Service Management (ITSM)

The ITIL (Information Technology Infrastructure Library) framework is a globally recognized set of best practices and guidelines for IT Service Management (ITSM). ITIL provides a structured approach to managing IT services, ensuring that they align with the needs of the business, are delivered efficiently, and consistently meet service quality standards. In this in-depth exploration, we will delve into the ITIL framework, its significance, core components, and best practices for effective ITSM.

1. Significance of the ITIL Framework:

1.1. Alignment with Business Objectives:

- **Strategic Focus:** ITIL helps organizations align their IT services with overall business goals and objectives, ensuring that technology investments support the achievement of strategic priorities.

- **Customer-Centricity:** ITIL emphasizes understanding and meeting the needs of customers and end-users, enhancing customer satisfaction and loyalty.

1.2. Operational Efficiency:

- **Process Standardization:** ITIL promotes the standardization of IT processes and practices, leading to increased operational efficiency and reduced risk of errors.

- **Resource Optimization:** By optimizing resource allocation and utilization, ITIL helps organizations control costs and make the most of available resources.

1.3. Service Quality and Continual Improvement:

- **Service Excellence:** ITIL focuses on delivering high-quality

IT services by defining service levels, monitoring performance, and continually improving service delivery.

- **Feedback Loops:** ITIL encourages organizations to collect feedback from users and stakeholders, using this information to drive improvements in service design and delivery.

2. Core Components of the ITIL Framework:

2.1. Service Strategy:

- **Defining Service Portfolios:** Identify and define the services an organization offers, including their value propositions, funding models, and strategic objectives.

- **Demand Management:** Anticipate and manage customer demand for services, aligning it with available resources.

2.2. Service Design:

- **Service Catalog Management:** Create and maintain a catalog of available services, including their descriptions, features, and service level agreements (SLAs).

- **Capacity Planning:** Ensure that IT resources are designed and provisioned to meet service demands.

- **Availability Management:** Maximize service availability by managing and mitigating risks.

- **Service Continuity Management:** Develop plans to maintain essential services in the event of disruptions or disasters.

2.3. Service Transition:

- **Change Management:** Control changes to IT services and systems to minimize service disruptions and risks.

- **Release and Deployment Management:** Plan, schedule, and manage the release of new services and updates.

- **Knowledge Management:** Capture, store, and share knowledge about IT services and their configurations.

2.4. Service Operation:

- **Incident Management:** Restore normal service operations as quickly as possible after incidents.

- **Problem Management:** Identify and address the root causes of recurring incidents.

- **Event Management:** Monitor IT infrastructure and services to detect and respond to events and potential issues.

- **Request Fulfillment:** Fulfill service requests efficiently and according to predefined procedures.

- **Access Management:** Ensure that only authorized users have access to IT services and data.

2.5. Continual Service Improvement (CSI):

- **CSI Approach:** Establish a culture of continual improvement by regularly assessing services, processes, and performance.

- **Metrics and KPIs:** Define and measure key performance indicators (KPIs) to gauge the success of improvement initiatives.

3. Best Practices for Effective ITSM Using ITIL:

3.1. Define Clear Service Levels:

- Clearly define SLAs, including response times, resolution times, and performance metrics.

- Communicate SLAs to customers and ensure that service teams are aware of their responsibilities.

3.2. Implement Change Control:

- Establish a rigorous change management process to evaluate, approve, and implement changes while minimizing risks.

3.3. Invest in Knowledge Management:

- Create a knowledge base to document solutions to common issues and empower support teams with readily available information.

3.4. Automate Routine Tasks:

- Implement automation for repetitive and routine tasks to improve efficiency and reduce human error.

3.5. Continuous Learning and Training:

- Invest in the training and development of IT staff to ensure they are equipped with the necessary skills to support ITIL practices.

3.6. Regularly Review and Update Processes:

- Continuously assess ITIL processes and adapt them to changing business needs and technology trends.

In conclusion, the ITIL framework serves as a comprehensive guide for organizations seeking to improve their ITSM practices. By embracing ITIL's best practices and principles, organizations can enhance their service quality, align IT with business objectives, optimize operational efficiency, and foster a culture of continual improvement. ITIL provides a structured and flexible framework that empowers organizations to adapt to the evolving landscape of technology and business, ensuring that their IT services remain agile, customer-focused, and responsive to changing demands.

B. Service Catalog Management in IT Service Management (ITSM)

Service Catalog Management is a crucial component of IT Service Management (ITSM) that focuses on defining, documenting, and delivering IT services to meet the needs of an organization and its customers. It serves as a structured and user-friendly interface between the IT department and its users, providing transparency, accountability, and efficiency in service delivery. In this in-depth exploration, we will delve into the significance of Service Catalog Management, its core elements, best practices, and its pivotal role in enhancing IT service quality and alignment with business objectives.

1. Significance of Service Catalog Management:

1.1. Customer-Centric Service Delivery:

- **User-Focused:** Service catalogs are designed with the end-users in mind, making it easier for them to request and access IT services that align with their specific needs and preferences.

- **Transparency:** Service catalogs provide transparency into available services, their features, associated costs, and service levels, fostering trust and confidence among users.

1.2. Standardization and Efficiency:

- **Consistency:** Service Catalog Management promotes the

standardization of service offerings and associated processes, ensuring that services are delivered consistently and in compliance with established standards.

- **Resource Optimization:** By defining and documenting services, service catalogs help organizations optimize resource allocation, reducing inefficiencies and waste.

1.3. Alignment with Business Objectives:

- **Strategic Mapping:** Service catalogs link IT services directly to the organization's strategic objectives, helping IT departments prioritize and deliver services that contribute to overall business goals.

- **Cost Visibility:** They provide visibility into the costs associated with each service, enabling organizations to make informed decisions about resource allocation and investment.

2. Core Elements of Service Catalog Management:

2.1. Service Definitions:

- **Service Descriptions:** Detailed descriptions of each IT service, including its purpose, features, and functionality.

- **Service Owners:** Identification of responsible individuals or teams accountable for delivering and maintaining each service.

2.2. Service Categorization:

- **Service Categories:** Grouping services into logical categories or portfolios based on their functionality or business relevance.

- **Taxonomy:** Establishing a structured hierarchy for services within categories for easy navigation.

2.3. Service Attributes:

- **Service Levels:** Defining service levels, including response times, resolution times, and availability targets.

- **Service Costs:** Documenting the cost of each service, including any associated fees or charges.

- **Dependencies:** Identifying any dependencies between services, ensuring that changes or disruptions in one service do not adversely affect others.

2.4. Request and Fulfillment Processes:

- **Service Request Forms:** Creating user-friendly request forms or portals that facilitate the submission of service requests.

- **Approval Workflows:** Defining approval processes for requests that require authorization.

- **Automated Fulfillment:** Implementing automation to

streamline service provisioning and delivery.

2.5. Service Catalog Access:

- **User Portals:** Providing a user-friendly web portal or interface where customers can browse the catalog, view service details, and request services.

- **Service Catalog Governance:** Ensuring that access to the service catalog is controlled and that only authorized users can make requests.

3. Best Practices for Effective Service Catalog Management:

3.1. Collaboration and Stakeholder Involvement:

- Collaborate with business units and departments to understand their service needs and expectations.

- Involve service owners and subject matter experts in defining and documenting service attributes.

3.2. Regular Updates and Maintenance:

- Continuously review and update the service catalog to reflect changes in services, service levels, or costs.

- Ensure that service owners are responsible for keeping their service definitions up to date.

3.3. User Training and Awareness:

- Provide training and guidance to users on how to navigate the service catalog and make service requests.

- Promote awareness of the service catalog's benefits and its role in improving service delivery.

3.4. Metrics and Reporting:

- Implement metrics and reporting mechanisms to track service catalog usage, request volumes, and customer satisfaction.

- Use data and feedback to identify areas for improvement and optimization.

3.5. Integration with ITSM Processes:

- Ensure seamless integration of the service catalog with other ITSM processes such as Incident Management, Change Management, and Service Level Management.

- Use the service catalog to facilitate incident reporting, change requests, and service level monitoring.

In conclusion, Service Catalog Management is a pivotal component of ITSM that enhances service delivery by providing a structured and user-friendly interface for IT services. It promotes transparency, standardization, and alignment with business objectives, ultimately improving the efficiency of IT departments and the satisfaction of their users. By defining, documenting, and continually updating services and their attributes, organizations can optimize resource allocation, reduce costs, and ensure that IT services contribute strategically to the overall success of the business.

C. Incident, Problem, and Change Management in IT Service Management (ITSM)

Incident, Problem, and Change Management are integral components of IT Service Management (ITSM) that collectively ensure the availability, reliability, and continuous improvement of IT services. These processes help organizations respond to and resolve incidents, identify and address underlying problems, and implement controlled changes to their IT environment. In this in-depth exploration, we will delve into the significance of Incident, Problem, and Change Management, their core elements, best practices, and how they work in tandem to enhance IT service quality and reliability.

1. Significance of Incident, Problem, and Change Management:

1.1. Incident Management:

- **Service Restoration:** Incident Management focuses on

swiftly restoring normal service operations following disruptions or incidents.

- **Customer Satisfaction:** Efficient incident resolution enhances customer satisfaction by minimizing service downtime and disruptions.

1.2. Problem Management:

- **Root Cause Analysis:** Problem Management delves deeper into recurring incidents, identifying their root causes and implementing permanent solutions.

- **Proactive Approach:** By addressing underlying problems, organizations can prevent incidents from recurring and improve overall service reliability.

1.3. Change Management:

- **Risk Mitigation:** Change Management ensures that all changes, whether software updates, hardware deployments, or configuration changes, are implemented in a controlled and risk-aware manner.

- **Minimizing Disruption:** It minimizes the risk of service disruptions and outages caused by unauthorized or poorly planned changes.

- **Continuous Improvement:** Change Management fosters a

culture of continual improvement by ensuring that changes are assessed, tested, and aligned with business objectives.

2. Core Elements of Incident, Problem, and Change Management:

2.1. Incident Management:

- **Incident Recording:** Logging all incidents, including details such as the incident's impact, urgency, and affected services.

- **Classification and Prioritization:** Categorizing incidents based on their impact and urgency to prioritize resolution efforts.

- **Incident Assignment:** Assigning incidents to appropriate support teams or individuals for investigation and resolution.

- **Resolution and Closure:** Swiftly resolving incidents and closing them after verification.

2.2. Problem Management:

- **Problem Identification:** Identifying recurring incidents and patterns of issues that may indicate underlying problems.

- **Root Cause Analysis:** Investigating and analyzing the root causes of problems to prevent them from recurring.

- **Workarounds:** Implementing temporary workarounds to

minimize the impact of known problems while permanent solutions are developed.

- **Problem Closure:** Closing problem records after successful resolution and documenting lessons learned.

2.3. Change Management:

- **Change Request Submission:** Receiving and documenting requests for changes, including their scope, impact, and business justification.

- **Change Evaluation:** Assessing the potential impact and risks associated with proposed changes.

- **Change Approval:** Gaining approval from a Change Advisory Board (CAB) or change authority before implementing changes.

- **Change Implementation:** Carrying out the approved changes while minimizing disruption and ensuring that rollback plans are in place.

- **Change Documentation:** Documenting and updating the configuration management database (CMDB) to reflect the new state of IT assets.

- **Post-implementation Review:** Evaluating the success and impact of changes after implementation and making adjustments as necessary.

3. Best Practices for Effective Incident, Problem, and Change Management:

3.1. Integration and Collaboration:

- Ensure seamless integration between Incident, Problem, and Change Management processes to facilitate communication and knowledge sharing.

- Foster collaboration between support teams, problem managers, and change managers to address issues comprehensively.

3.2. Incident Prioritization:

- Implement a clear and consistent incident prioritization scheme based on agreed-upon criteria, ensuring that critical incidents receive prompt attention.

3.3. Problem Analysis:

- Conduct thorough root cause analysis for recurring incidents to identify and address underlying problems effectively.

- Use tools and techniques such as the "5 Whys" or fishbone diagrams to explore the causes of problems.

3.4. Change Testing:

- Develop comprehensive testing plans for changes, including rollback procedures and testing in a controlled environment before production deployment.

- Use automated testing tools to streamline the testing process.

3.5. Change Communication:

- Communicate planned changes to all relevant stakeholders well in advance, providing information about the change's purpose, potential impact, and timing.

- Establish clear channels for stakeholders to report concerns or feedback related to changes.

3.6. Continuous Improvement:

- Regularly review incident, problem, and change data to identify trends, areas for improvement, and opportunities to enhance service quality.

- Implement improvements based on data-driven insights and feedback from stakeholders.

In conclusion, Incident, Problem, and Change Management are critical processes within ITSM that collectively ensure the reliability and continuous improvement of IT services. Incident Management focuses on rapid resolution, Problem Management identifies and addresses root causes, and Change Management ensures controlled and risk-aware changes. When executed effectively and collaboratively, these processes enhance service quality, minimize disruptions, and contribute to the overall success of an organization by aligning IT services with business objectives and fostering a culture of continual improvement.

D. Service Desk Operations in IT Service Management (ITSM)

Service Desk Operations serve as the frontline of IT support and communication between IT departments and end-users or customers. They play a crucial role in IT Service Management (ITSM) by providing a centralized point of contact for incident reporting, service requests, and user inquiries. In this in-depth exploration, we will delve into the significance of Service Desk Operations, their core elements, best practices, and their pivotal role in ensuring efficient IT service delivery and user satisfaction.

1. Significance of Service Desk Operations:

1.1. Single Point of Contact:

- **User Convenience:** The Service Desk serves as a single, user-friendly interface for all IT-related inquiries and support needs.

- **Efficiency:** It streamlines communication and reduces the complexity of accessing IT services or reporting issues.

1.2. Incident Resolution and Service Requests:

- **Rapid Response:** Service Desk teams are responsible for promptly acknowledging incidents and service requests, facilitating swift resolution.

- **Resource Allocation:** They prioritize and assign incidents to appropriate support teams or individuals for efficient resolution.

1.3. User Satisfaction and Feedback:

- **User Experience:** Service Desks aim to enhance user satisfaction by providing responsive, helpful, and professional support.

- **Feedback Loop:** They gather user feedback to identify areas for improvement and enhance IT service quality.

2. Core Elements of Service Desk Operations:

2.1. Incident Logging and Classification:

- **User Interaction:** Interacting with users to gather incident details, classify incidents, and create incident records.

- **Priority Determination:** Assessing the impact and urgency of incidents to prioritize their resolution.

2.2. Incident Triage and Assignment:

- **Triage:** Determining the severity and complexity of incidents to allocate appropriate resources.

- **Assignment:** Assigning incidents to support agents or teams based on their expertise and availability.

2.3. Incident Resolution and Escalation:

- **Resolution:** Working on incidents to restore normal service operation as quickly as possible.

- **Escalation:** Escalating incidents to higher-level support or management when required by incident severity or complexity.

2.4. Service Request Fulfillment:

- **User Requests:** Handling service requests, such as password resets, software installations, and hardware provisioning.

- **Request Tracking:** Monitoring and tracking the progress of service requests to ensure timely fulfillment.

2.5. Knowledge Management:

- **Knowledge Base:** Maintaining a knowledge base that contains solutions, FAQs, and troubleshooting guides for common issues.

- **Self-Service:** Encouraging users to utilize self-service options within the knowledge base for quick issue resolution.

2.6. User Communication and Feedback:

- **Communication:** Keeping users informed about incident or service request status, progress, and resolutions.

- **Feedback Collection:** Collecting feedback from users regarding their service desk experiences and incorporating it into service improvement initiatives.

2.7. Performance Metrics and Reporting:

- **Key Performance Indicators (KPIs):** Tracking KPIs such as response times, resolution times, and user satisfaction to measure service desk performance.

- **Reporting:** Generating reports and analytics to assess service desk efficiency and identify areas for improvement.

3. Best Practices for Effective Service Desk Operations:

3.1. Service Desk Staff Training:

- Provide comprehensive training and ongoing professional development for service desk staff to enhance technical skills and customer service capabilities.

3.2. Implement Service Desk Tools:

- Utilize ITSM software tools to streamline incident and request management, automate workflows, and improve communication and reporting.

3.3. Follow ITIL Best Practices:

- Align Service Desk Operations with ITIL best practices, ensuring that incident, request, and problem management processes are well-defined and consistent.

3.4. Continual Improvement:

- Foster a culture of continuous improvement by regularly reviewing incident data, user feedback, and performance metrics to identify and address service desk bottlenecks or inefficiencies.

3.5. Self-Service Options:

- Promote self-service options and empower users to resolve common issues independently using the knowledge base or self-help guides.

3.6. Effective Communication:

- Maintain clear and responsive communication with users, setting expectations for incident resolution and keeping users informed of progress.

3.7. Incident Prioritization:

- Implement a clear incident prioritization scheme based on agreed-upon criteria, ensuring that critical incidents receive prompt attention.

3.8. User Feedback Integration:

- Actively incorporate user feedback into service desk improvement initiatives, ensuring that service quality continually evolves to meet user expectations.

In conclusion, Service Desk Operations are a critical component of ITSM that bridge the gap between IT departments and end-users or customers. They are the first line of support, responsible for incident resolution, service request fulfillment, and user communication. When executed effectively and in alignment with best practices, Service Desk Operations contribute to user satisfaction, efficient IT service delivery, and a culture of continuous improvement within ITSM.

E. Key Performance Indicators (KPIs) in IT Service Management (ITSM)

Key Performance Indicators (KPIs) are vital metrics that organizations use to assess the effectiveness, efficiency, and quality of their IT Service Management (ITSM) processes. KPIs provide valuable insights into the performance of ITSM practices, helping organizations make data-driven decisions, enhance service delivery, and align IT with business goals. In this in-depth exploration, we will delve into the significance of KPIs in ITSM, common KPI categories, specific KPI examples, and best practices for their implementation.

1. Significance of KPIs in ITSM:

1.1. Performance Assessment:

- **Continuous Improvement:** KPIs provide a means to assess the current performance of ITSM processes and identify areas for improvement.

- **Benchmarking:** They enable organizations to benchmark their performance against industry standards and best practices.

1.2. Alignment with Business Objectives:

- **Strategic Alignment:** KPIs help ensure that ITSM efforts align with the strategic objectives and priorities of the organization.

- **Resource Allocation:** They assist in allocating resources effectively by focusing on areas that contribute most to business success.

1.3. Accountability and Transparency:

- **Accountability:** KPIs promote accountability by measuring the performance of teams and individuals responsible for ITSM processes.

- **Transparency:** They provide transparency to stakeholders, including senior management and customers, regarding the quality of IT services.

2. Common Categories of KPIs in ITSM:

2.1. Service Desk and Incident Management KPIs:

- **First Call Resolution Rate:** The percentage of incidents resolved during the initial user contact.

- **Average Response Time:** The average time it takes for support teams to respond to incidents.

- **Incident Closure Rate:** The percentage of incidents successfully closed within agreed-upon timeframes.

2.2. Change Management KPIs:

- **Change Success Rate:** The percentage of changes implemented successfully without causing disruptions.

- **Change Lead Time:** The average time it takes to implement approved changes.

- **Emergency Change Volume:** The number of unplanned emergency changes, indicating potential operational issues.

2.3. Problem Management KPIs:

- **Root Cause Identification Rate:** The percentage of problems for which the root cause is successfully identified.

- **Problem Resolution Time:** The average time it takes to resolve problems and prevent incidents from recurring.

- **Number of Known Errors:** The count of known errors that have been identified and documented.

2.4. Service Level Management KPIs:

- **Service Availability:** The percentage of time that services are available and operational.

- **Service Level Agreement (SLA) Compliance:** The percentage of SLAs met within agreed-upon parameters.

- **Service Satisfaction Score:** User or customer satisfaction scores related to specific IT services.

2.5. Change Request and Release Management KPIs:

- **Release Defect Rate:** The percentage of defects or issues identified in releases after deployment.

- **Change Request Backlog:** The number of pending change

requests awaiting approval or implementation.

- **Change Rollback Rate:** The percentage of changes requiring rollback due to issues or failures.

2.6. Knowledge Management and Self-Service KPIs:

- **Knowledge Base Utilization:** The percentage of incidents or requests resolved using knowledge base articles.

- **User Adoption of Self-Service:** The percentage of users utilizing self-service options for issue resolution.

3. Best Practices for Implementing KPIs in ITSM:

3.1. Define Clear Objectives:

- Clearly define the objectives and purpose of each KPI to ensure alignment with business goals.

3.2. Select Relevant KPIs:

- Choose KPIs that are relevant to the specific ITSM processes and align with organizational priorities.

3.3. Establish Baselines:

- Establish baseline measurements to track changes in performance over time and assess the impact of improvement initiatives.

3.4. Set Targets and Thresholds:

- Define targets and thresholds for each KPI to establish performance expectations and trigger actions when thresholds are breached.

3.5. Automate Data Collection:

- Implement automation and ITSM tools to collect and analyze KPI data, reducing manual effort and improving accuracy.

3.6. Regular Monitoring and Reporting:

- Continuously monitor KPIs and generate regular reports to track progress and share insights with stakeholders.

3.7. Root Cause Analysis:

- Conduct root cause analysis for KPI deviations to identify underlying issues and drive corrective actions.

3.8. Foster a Culture of Improvement:

- Encourage teams to use KPI data to drive improvement initiatives and continually enhance ITSM processes.

In conclusion, KPIs are instrumental in evaluating and enhancing the performance of ITSM processes. By measuring and analyzing key metrics across various ITSM areas, organizations can gain valuable insights into service quality, efficiency, and alignment with business objectives. The implementation of KPIs, when coupled with a commitment to continual improvement, helps organizations optimize ITSM practices, deliver superior IT services, and maintain a competitive edge in today's technology-driven landscape.

CHAPTER 5

Infrastructure as Code (IaC) and Automation

In the ever-evolving landscape of information technology, Infrastructure as Code (IaC) and automation stand as transformative paradigms reshaping the way organizations manage and deploy their IT resources. IaC represents a revolutionary approach to provisioning and configuring infrastructure using code and automation scripts, while automation itself is a fundamental pillar in streamlining IT operations. In this introductory exploration, we embark on a journey into the realm of IaC and automation, unraveling their significance, principles, benefits, and their pivotal role in driving efficiency, scalability, and agility in the world of IT infrastructure management.

A. Understanding Infrastructure as Code (IaC) Principles

Infrastructure as Code (IaC) is a methodology that revolutionizes the management of IT infrastructure by treating it as code. IaC enables organizations to provision, configure, and manage infrastructure resources using code, scripts, and automation tools. This approach provides numerous benefits, including enhanced agility, scalability, and consistency. In this in-depth exploration, we will delve into the principles that underpin IaC, its significance, and how it transforms the way IT infrastructure is managed.

1. Codification of Infrastructure:

1.1. Declarative vs. Imperative: IaC allows infrastructure to be defined in a declarative manner, specifying the desired end state without detailing the procedural steps to achieve it. This differs from the imperative approach, where specific instructions for each operation are provided.

1.2. Infrastructure as Data: IaC treats infrastructure components (servers, networks, storage, etc.) as data. These resources are defined and manipulated through code, making infrastructure management more akin to software development.

2. Version Control:

2.1. Code Repository: IaC code is stored in a version control system (e.g., Git). This enables tracking changes, collaboration among teams, and the ability to roll back to previous configurations if needed.

2.2. Immutable Infrastructure: IaC promotes the concept of immutable infrastructure, where changes to infrastructure are achieved by creating new instances rather than modifying existing ones. Version control ensures reproducibility and consistency.

3. Automation and Orchestration:

3.1. Scripted Automation: IaC relies on scripts and automation tools to perform infrastructure tasks. This automation eliminates manual, error-prone configurations and reduces the risk of misconfigurations.

3.2. Orchestrated Workflows: IaC enables the orchestration of complex workflows involving multiple infrastructure components. Dependencies and sequencing of actions are defined in code.

4. Reusability and Modularity:

4.1. Modular Components: Infrastructure components are defined as reusable modules. For example, a web server module can be reused across various projects with minor adjustments.

4.2. Parameterization: IaC code often includes parameters that allow customization for different environments, such as development, testing, and production.

5. Idempotency:

5.1. Idempotent Operations: IaC operations are designed to be idempotent, meaning that running the same operation multiple times has the same result as running it once. This reduces the risk of unintended changes.

6. Testing and Validation:

6.1. Automated Testing: IaC code can be subjected to automated testing to validate its correctness. This includes testing for syntax errors, code linting, and functional testing of infrastructure changes.

6.2. Continuous Integration (CI): IaC can be integrated into CI/CD pipelines, allowing infrastructure changes to be automatically tested, validated, and deployed in a controlled and consistent manner.

7. Change Management:

7.1. Controlled Changes: IaC promotes controlled changes to infrastructure through versioning and change management processes. Changes are tracked, reviewed, and approved before deployment.

7.2. Rollback Capabilities: The ability to roll back to previous infrastructure states ensures that if issues arise during deployment, the system can be reverted to a known, working state.

8. Scalability and Elasticity:

8.1. Dynamic Scaling: IaC enables dynamic scaling of resources in response to changes in demand. Scaling policies can be defined in code and triggered automatically.

8.2. Cost Optimization: IaC allows organizations to provision resources on-demand, optimizing costs by scaling up or down as needed.

9. Security and Compliance:

9.1. Security as Code: Security configurations can be defined in code, ensuring that security measures are consistently applied to all infrastructure components.

9.2. Compliance Checks: IaC can include compliance checks and controls, allowing organizations to enforce regulatory and security policies automatically.

10. Documentation and Self-Service:

10.1. Self-Documenting: IaC code serves as documentation for infrastructure, making it easier for teams to understand, maintain, and troubleshoot.

10.2. Self-Service Portals: IaC can be integrated into self-service portals, enabling teams to provision and manage infrastructure resources autonomously.

In conclusion, Infrastructure as Code (IaC) represents a paradigm shift in IT infrastructure management, emphasizing automation, version control, and the codification of infrastructure components. By adhering to these principles, organizations can achieve greater agility, reliability, and consistency in their infrastructure operations. IaC empowers IT teams to treat infrastructure like software, making it more manageable, scalable, and adaptable to the ever-evolving needs of modern businesses.

B. Tools and Technologies for Infrastructure as Code (IaC)

Infrastructure as Code (IaC) relies on a variety of tools and technologies to automate the provisioning and management of IT infrastructure using code and scripts. These tools play a critical role in enabling organizations to achieve the benefits of IaC, such as efficiency, scalability, and consistency. In this in-depth exploration, we will delve into the essential tools and technologies used in IaC, how they work, and their significance in modern IT infrastructure management.

1. Configuration Management Tools:

1.1. Ansible:

- **Purpose:** Ansible automates configuration management, application deployment, and task automation.

- **Key Features:** Agentless architecture, idempotent modules, extensive library of pre-built roles.

1.2. Puppet:

- **Purpose:** Puppet automates the configuration and management of infrastructure components.

- **Key Features:** Declarative language (Puppet DSL), Puppet Forge for reusable modules, support for Windows and Linux.

1.3. Chef:

- **Purpose:** Chef automates infrastructure provisioning and configuration management.

- **Key Features:** Infrastructure as Code (Ruby DSL), Chef Supermarket for cookbooks, support for cloud platforms.

2. Orchestration and Provisioning Tools:

2.1. Terraform:

- **Purpose:** Terraform provides infrastructure provisioning using a declarative configuration language.

- **Key Features:** Multi-cloud support, infrastructure as code, resource dependency management.

2.2. AWS CloudFormation:

- **Purpose:** AWS CloudFormation automates the provisioning of AWS resources.

- **Key Features:** Templates in JSON or YAML, stack creation and management, resource dependencies.

2.3. Azure Resource Manager (ARM) Templates:

- **Purpose:** ARM Templates automate the deployment and management of Azure resources.

- **Key Features:** JSON templates, declarative language, resource grouping.

3. Container Orchestration:

3.1. Kubernetes:

- **Purpose:** Kubernetes automates the deployment, scaling, and management of containerized applications.

- **Key Features:** Container orchestration, declarative YAML configuration, scaling and load balancing.

4. Configuration Version Control:

4.1. Git:

- **Purpose:** Git is a distributed version control system used for tracking changes in IaC code.

- **Key Features:** Branching and merging, collaboration, code history tracking.

5. Continuous Integration and Continuous Deployment (CI/CD):

5.1. Jenkins:

- **Purpose:** Jenkins automates the building, testing, and deployment of IaC code and applications.

- **Key Features:** Extensive plugin ecosystem, pipeline as code, integration with version control systems.

5.2. CircleCI:

- **Purpose:** CircleCI automates the CI/CD process for IaC projects.

- **Key Features:** Configuration in YAML, parallelism, integration with various cloud providers.

6. Cloud Services:

6.1. AWS CloudFormation:

- **Purpose:** AWS CloudFormation provides native IaC capabilities for AWS resources.

- **Key Features:** Template-based provisioning, AWS-specific resource management.

6.2. Google Cloud Deployment Manager:

- **Purpose:** Google Cloud Deployment Manager automates the provisioning of Google Cloud Platform resources.

- **Key Features:** Configuration in YAML or Jinja2, resource dependencies.

7. Infrastructure as Code IDEs and Editors:

7.1. Visual Studio Code (VS Code):

- **Purpose:** VS Code is a popular code editor with extensions for IaC languages and tools.

- **Key Features:** Syntax highlighting, debugging, extensions for popular IaC tools.

7.2. JetBrains IDEs (e.g., PyCharm, IntelliJ):

- **Purpose:** JetBrains IDEs support IaC languages and offer code completion and debugging features.

- **Key Features:** Intelligent code analysis, support for various programming languages.

8. Monitoring and Logging:

8.1. Prometheus and Grafana:

- **Purpose:** Prometheus is an open-source monitoring and

alerting toolkit, while Grafana is a visualization tool for monitoring data.

- **Key Features:** Metric collection, alerting, visualization.

8.2. ELK Stack (Elasticsearch, Logstash, Kibana):

- **Purpose:** ELK Stack provides centralized logging and log analysis.

- **Key Features:** Log collection, parsing, search, and visualization.

In conclusion, the tools and technologies for Infrastructure as Code (IaC) play a vital role in automating and managing IT infrastructure. These tools offer diverse capabilities, from configuration management and provisioning to container orchestration and continuous integration. By leveraging the right combination of IaC tools and technologies, organizations can streamline infrastructure operations, enhance agility, and maintain the consistency and reliability of their IT environments.

C. Automation in IT Infrastructure Management

Automation in IT infrastructure management represents a pivotal shift in the way organizations design, deploy, and maintain their IT environments. It involves the use of technology and processes to replace manual, repetitive tasks with efficient, consistent, and error-free automated processes. This transformative approach not only saves time and reduces operational costs but also enhances scalability, agility, and overall infrastructure reliability. In this in-depth exploration, we will delve into the principles, benefits, key components, and best practices of automation in IT infrastructure management.

1. Principles of Automation in IT Infrastructure Management:

1.1. Efficiency and Consistency: Automation eliminates human errors and ensures that repetitive tasks are performed consistently, leading to reliable and predictable infrastructure operations.

1.2. Scalability: Automated processes can easily scale to accommodate increased workloads or infrastructure expansion without a proportional increase in human effort.

1.3. Speed: Automation accelerates tasks that would take hours or days if done manually, enabling rapid response to changing business requirements.

1.4. Risk Reduction: Automation reduces the risk of configuration drift, security vulnerabilities, and human-induced errors, enhancing infrastructure stability and security.

2. Benefits of Automation in IT Infrastructure Management:

2.1. Cost Savings: Reduced labor costs, efficient resource utilization, and fewer errors translate into significant cost savings over time.

2.2. Improved Reliability: Automated processes are highly reliable, minimizing service disruptions and downtime.

2.3. Agility: Automation enables IT teams to respond quickly to changing business needs, adapt to market demands, and implement changes without delays.

2.4. Enhanced Security: Automation can enforce security policies consistently across the entire infrastructure, reducing vulnerabilities and ensuring compliance.

2.5. Scalability: Automated infrastructure can scale up or down seamlessly to accommodate fluctuating workloads.

3. Key Components of Automation in IT Infrastructure Management:

3.1. Scripting and Coding: Writing scripts or code to automate tasks and processes is fundamental to automation in IT infrastructure management. Scripting languages like Python, PowerShell, and Ruby are commonly used.

3.2. Configuration Management: Tools like Ansible, Puppet, and Chef automate the configuration and management of servers and other infrastructure components.

3.3. Orchestration: Orchestration tools, such as Kubernetes and Docker Swarm, automate the deployment and management of containerized applications.

3.4. Continuous Integration and Continuous Deployment (CI/CD): CI/CD pipelines automate the testing, integration, and deployment of applications and infrastructure changes.

3.5. Monitoring and Alerting: Automated monitoring tools like Prometheus and Nagios detect issues in real-time and trigger automated responses or alerts.

3.6. Self-Service Portals: Self-service portals enable users to request and provision resources autonomously within defined policies and workflows.

3.7. Cloud Services and APIs: Cloud providers offer APIs and automation services that allow users to automate the provisioning and management of cloud resources.

4. Best Practices for Automation in IT Infrastructure Management:

4.1. Comprehensive Planning: Develop a clear automation strategy that aligns with business goals and IT infrastructure requirements.

4.2. Start Small: Begin with automating routine, repetitive tasks before moving on to more complex processes.

4.3. Standardization: Establish standardized configurations and templates for infrastructure components to simplify automation.

4.4. Version Control: Apply version control to automation scripts and code to track changes and ensure reproducibility.

4.5. Testing: Implement automated testing procedures to validate the correctness and reliability of automation scripts and processes.

4.6. Documentation: Document automation processes and workflows to facilitate troubleshooting and knowledge sharing.

4.7. Monitoring and Governance: Implement automated monitoring and governance mechanisms to track the performance and compliance of automated processes.

4.8. Collaboration: Foster collaboration between development and operations teams to ensure that automation aligns with application requirements.

In conclusion, automation in IT infrastructure management is a transformative approach that enhances efficiency, reliability, scalability, and agility in IT operations. By adhering to automation principles, organizations can leverage the full potential of automation tools and technologies to streamline infrastructure management, reduce costs, and respond rapidly to evolving business needs. Automation is not merely a technological advancement but a strategic imperative for organizations aiming to stay competitive in a rapidly changing digital landscape.

D. Continuous Integration and Continuous Deployment (CI/CD)

Continuous Integration and Continuous Deployment (CI/CD) is a set of practices and principles that revolutionize software development and delivery by automating and streamlining the building, testing, and deployment of applications. CI/CD aims to shorten the software development lifecycle, increase collaboration between development and operations teams, and enhance the speed, quality, and reliability of software releases. In this in-depth exploration, we will delve into the core concepts, benefits, key components, and best practices of CI/CD.

1. Core Concepts of CI/CD:

1.1. Continuous Integration (CI):

- **Purpose:** CI involves the frequent integration of code changes into a shared repository, where automated tests are run to detect integration issues.

- **Benefits:** Early bug detection, code quality improvement, faster development cycles.

1.2. Continuous Deployment (CD):

- **Purpose:** CD extends CI by automating the deployment of code changes to production or staging environments after successful testing.

- **Benefits:** Rapid and reliable releases, reduced manual intervention, consistent deployments.

1.3. Pipeline Automation:

- **Pipeline:** CI/CD pipelines automate the stages of building, testing, and deploying applications, ensuring that each code change follows the same process.

- **Automation:** Automation scripts and tools orchestrate the pipeline, reducing human intervention and potential errors.

1.4. Version Control:

- **Version Control System (VCS):** CI/CD relies on a VCS like Git to track code changes, maintain version history, and enable collaboration.

- **Branching Strategies:** Branches are used for isolating

features, bug fixes, and releases, ensuring a structured development process.

2. Benefits of CI/CD:

2.1. Faster Time-to-Market:

- CI/CD accelerates the delivery of new features and bug fixes, enabling organizations to respond quickly to user needs and market changes.

2.2. Reduced Risk:

- Automated testing and deployment minimize human errors, leading to more reliable and consistent software releases.

2.3. Improved Collaboration:

- CI/CD promotes collaboration between development, testing, and operations teams, fostering a culture of shared responsibility.

2.4. Increased Quality:

- Continuous testing ensures that code changes do not introduce regressions or degrade application quality.

2.5. Resource Efficiency:

- Automation reduces manual effort and allows teams to allocate resources more effectively.

2.6. Enhanced Feedback Loop:

- Rapid feedback from automated tests and deployments enables quicker issue resolution and iterative development.

3. Key Components of CI/CD:

3.1. Source Code Repository:

- A VCS, such as Git, serves as the central repository for version-controlled code.

3.2. Build Automation:

- Build tools like Jenkins, Travis CI, or GitLab CI automate the compilation of source code into executable artifacts.

3.3. Automated Testing:

- Testing frameworks and tools (e.g., JUnit, Selenium) automate unit, integration, and end-to-end tests.

3.4. Deployment Automation:

- Deployment tools (e.g., Ansible, Docker, Kubernetes) automate the deployment and configuration of applications.

3.5. Orchestration and Pipeline Tools:

- CI/CD pipeline tools (e.g., Jenkins, CircleCI, GitLab CI/CD) orchestrate the automated stages of the development process.

3.6. Monitoring and Feedback:

- Monitoring and logging tools (e.g., Prometheus, ELK Stack) provide insights into application performance and issues.

4. Best Practices for CI/CD:

4.1. Automated Testing:

- Implement a comprehensive suite of automated tests, including unit, integration, and end-to-end tests.

4.2. Version Control:

- Enforce strict version control practices and use branching strategies to manage code changes.

4.3. Consistency Across Environments:

- Ensure that development, testing, and production environments are as similar as possible to reduce deployment issues.

4.4. Security Integration:

- Include security scans and checks in the CI/CD pipeline to identify vulnerabilities early in the development process.

4.5. Incremental Deployment:

- Deploy small, incremental changes to minimize risk and

enable faster rollbacks if issues arise.

4.6. Continuous Monitoring:

- Implement continuous monitoring to detect and address issues in real-time.

In conclusion, Continuous Integration and Continuous Deployment (CI/CD) is a transformative approach to software development and delivery that enhances speed, quality, and reliability while reducing risk. By automating key stages of the development process and promoting collaboration, organizations can achieve rapid, consistent, and efficient software releases, ultimately improving their ability to respond to customer needs and market demands. CI/CD is not just a technical practice but a cultural shift that fosters a mindset of continuous improvement and innovation in software development.

E. Benefits of Infrastructure as Code (IaC) and Automation

Infrastructure as Code (IaC) and automation are game-changing practices in IT infrastructure management. They offer a multitude of benefits that transform the way organizations build, manage, and scale their IT environments. In this in-depth exploration, we will delve into the myriad advantages of IaC and automation, from efficiency and scalability to reliability and cost savings.

1. Efficiency and Time Savings:

1.1. Rapid Provisioning: IaC allows for the quick and automated provisioning of infrastructure resources, reducing the time required to set up servers, networks, and other components.

1.2. Consistency: Automation ensures that configurations and deployments are consistent across environments, eliminating the need for manual adjustments and reducing errors.

1.3. Streamlined Operations: Automation scripts and tools automate routine tasks, freeing IT teams from repetitive, manual work and enabling them to focus on higher-value activities.

1.4. Faster Development Cycles: CI/CD pipelines, enabled by automation, accelerate development cycles, facilitating the rapid delivery of new features and bug fixes.

2. Scalability and Elasticity:

2.1. Dynamic Scaling: IaC and automation allow organizations to scale resources up or down based on demand, ensuring optimal resource utilization and cost efficiency.

2.2. Resource Optimization: Automation tools can monitor resource usage and automatically allocate or deallocate resources as needed, preventing over-provisioning.

3. Reliability and Consistency:

3.1. Reduced Human Error: Automation minimizes the risk of human-induced errors, ensuring consistent and reliable infrastructure configurations.

3.2. Predictable Deployments: IaC and automation result in predictable deployments, reducing the chances of configuration drift and unexpected issues.

3.3. Rollback Capabilities: Automation enables easy rollback to previous configurations in the event of issues or failures, ensuring service continuity.

4. Enhanced Security and Compliance:

4.1. Consistent Security Policies: Security configurations can be automated and consistently applied across the entire infrastructure, reducing security vulnerabilities.

4.2. Compliance Checks: IaC and automation can enforce compliance with industry regulations and internal policies through automated checks and controls.

4.3. Rapid Security Updates: Automation allows for the swift deployment of security updates and patches, reducing exposure to vulnerabilities.

5. Cost Savings:

5.1. Reduced Labor Costs: Automation decreases the need for manual intervention, leading to cost savings in terms of labor and operational expenses.

5.2. Efficient Resource Allocation: Automation optimizes resource allocation, preventing over-provisioning and unnecessary infrastructure costs.

5.3. Cloud Cost Control: IaC tools can optimize cloud resource usage, helping organizations manage cloud expenses effectively.

6. Collaboration and DevOps Culture:

6.1. Cross-Functional Collaboration: IaC and automation promote collaboration between development and operations teams, fostering a DevOps culture.

6.2. Shared Responsibility: DevOps teams share responsibility for the entire software delivery lifecycle, leading to improved communication and shared goals.

7. Disaster Recovery and Resilience:

7.1. Automated Backup and Recovery: Automation can handle backup and recovery processes, ensuring data integrity and minimal downtime during disasters.

7.2. High Availability: Automation can facilitate the setup of redundant and high-availability configurations, enhancing system resilience.

8. Flexibility and Portability:

8.1. Multi-Cloud Support: IaC and automation make it easier to deploy applications across multiple cloud providers, increasing flexibility and avoiding vendor lock-in.

8.2. Code Portability: IaC code can be versioned, making it transportable across environments and teams.

9. Monitoring and Analytics:

9.1. Real-Time Insights: Automation tools can integrate with monitoring and analytics platforms, providing real-time insights into infrastructure performance.

9.2. Data-Driven Decisions: Access to data and metrics allows organizations to make informed decisions, optimize resource allocation, and plan for growth.

In conclusion, Infrastructure as Code (IaC) and automation offer a multitude of benefits that are instrumental in modernizing IT infrastructure management. These practices enhance efficiency, scalability, reliability, and security while reducing operational costs and promoting collaboration among teams. IaC and automation are not only technical advancements but also cultural shifts that empower organizations to adapt and thrive in an increasingly digital and competitive landscape.

CHAPTER 6

Networking and Data Center Setup

Networking and data center setup represent the backbone of modern IT infrastructure, serving as the foundation upon which digital services, applications, and data are built and delivered. In today's interconnected world, the effective design, deployment, and management of network architecture and data center facilities are critical for organizations to achieve optimal performance, reliability, and security. In this introductory exploration, we embark on a journey into the realm of networking and data center setup, unraveling their significance, key components, and the pivotal role they play in supporting the ever-evolving demands of the digital age.

A. Selecting the Right Location for Networking and Data Center Setup

Choosing the right location for networking and data center setup is a critical decision that significantly impacts the performance, resilience, and cost-effectiveness of an organization's IT infrastructure. The location not only affects the accessibility to users and clients but also influences factors such as connectivity, security, scalability, and disaster recovery capabilities. In this in-depth exploration, we will delve into the considerations and best practices for selecting the optimal location for your networking and data center facilities.

1. Geographic Considerations:

1.1. Proximity to Users and Clients:

- The data center should be strategically located to minimize latency and ensure fast access to applications and services for end-users and clients.

- Consider the geographical distribution of your user base and the location of key clients.

1.2. Disaster Risk Assessment:

- Evaluate the region's susceptibility to natural disasters such as earthquakes, floods, hurricanes, and wildfires.

- Select a location with a lower risk of these disasters or implement robust disaster recovery measures.

1.3. Redundancy and Geographical Diversity:

- Consider redundancy by establishing multiple data center sites in geographically diverse regions to ensure high availability and business continuity.

2. Connectivity and Network Infrastructure:

2.1. Proximity to Internet Exchange Points (IXPs):

- Locate data centers close to major IXPs to benefit from high-speed and low-latency connectivity to the internet and other networks.

2.2. Network Redundancy:

- Ensure multiple, diverse network connectivity options to prevent network outages and reduce reliance on a single provider.

2.3. Fiber Optic Availability:

- Assess the availability of fiber optic infrastructure in the area, as it is essential for high-speed data transmission.

3. Power and Cooling Infrastructure:

3.1. Access to Reliable Power Grids:

- Choose locations with reliable and stable power grids to minimize the risk of power interruptions.

- Consider backup power sources such as generators and uninterruptible power supplies (UPS).

3.2. Cooling Efficiency:

- Ensure adequate cooling facilities to maintain optimal operating temperatures for servers and networking equipment.

- Consider natural cooling options or advanced cooling technologies to enhance energy efficiency.

4. Security and Compliance:

4.1. Physical Security:

- Select locations with robust physical security measures, including controlled access, surveillance, and security personnel.

- Consider the proximity to law enforcement and emergency response services.

4.2. Regulatory and Compliance Requirements:

- Ensure that the chosen location complies with industry-specific regulations and data privacy laws.

- Consider certifications such as SOC 2, ISO 27001, and HIPAA, if applicable.

5. Scalability and Growth:

5.1. Space for Expansion:

- Choose a location that offers room for expansion as your IT infrastructure needs grow.

- Plan for additional racks, servers, and networking equipment.

5.2. Access to Skilled Workforce:

- Evaluate the availability of skilled IT professionals in the area who can support your data center operations and networking needs.

6. Cost Considerations:

6.1. Operational Costs:

- Assess the overall cost of operations in the selected location, including real estate, utilities, and labor.

- Compare costs with the expected benefits and ROI.

6.2. Tax Incentives:

- Investigate tax incentives or benefits offered by the local government to reduce operational costs.

7. Future-Proofing:

7.1. Technology Trends:

- Consider emerging technologies such as edge computing and 5G when selecting the location to ensure future compatibility.

7.2. Vendor and Service Provider Presence:

- Evaluate the presence of major technology vendors and service providers in the area, which can facilitate future partnerships and support.

In conclusion, selecting the right location for networking and data center setup requires a comprehensive assessment of geographic, infrastructure, security, and cost-related factors. It's a strategic decision that should align with your organization's business goals, IT requirements, and long-term growth plans. By carefully considering these factors, organizations can ensure that their data center and networking facilities are well-positioned to meet current and future needs while minimizing risks and optimizing performance.

B. Power and Cooling Requirements for Networking and Data Center Setup

Power and cooling are foundational elements of any networking and data center setup. They play a crucial role in ensuring the reliability, efficiency, and performance of IT infrastructure. In this in-depth exploration, we will delve into the key considerations and best practices for managing power and cooling requirements in a data center environment.

1. Power Requirements:

1.1. Load Analysis:

- Begin by conducting a thorough analysis of the power requirements of your IT equipment. This includes servers, networking gear, storage devices, and other components.

- Identify both the peak and average power consumption for each piece of equipment.

1.2. Redundancy and Reliability:

- Consider the level of redundancy required for power sources to minimize the risk of downtime. Common redundancy configurations include N+1 and 2N setups.

- Implement uninterruptible power supplies (UPS) to provide temporary power during outages and ensure graceful shutdowns.

1.3. Power Distribution:

- Plan for adequate power distribution units (PDUs) and ensure they are properly balanced to prevent overloading.

- Implement power monitoring and management solutions to track power consumption and identify anomalies.

1.4. Energy Efficiency:

- Optimize energy efficiency through practices such as hot and cold aisle containment, efficient power supplies, and the use of energy-efficient hardware.

- Consider renewable energy sources, such as solar or wind power, to reduce the environmental impact.

2. Cooling Requirements:

2.1. Heat Load Calculation:

- Calculate the heat load generated by IT equipment. This includes both sensible heat (directly affecting temperature) and latent heat (humidity control).

- Use industry-standard formulas or thermal assessment tools to perform heat load calculations.

2.2. Cooling System Design:

- Choose an appropriate cooling system based on the heat load and the data center's layout. Common cooling systems include precision air conditioning, in-row cooling, and hot/cold aisle containment.

- Implement a well-designed airflow management strategy to ensure efficient cooling distribution.

2.3. Temperature and Humidity Control:

- Maintain temperature and humidity levels within recommended ranges to optimize equipment performance and reliability.

- Deploy environmental monitoring systems to track and alert staff to deviations from optimal conditions.

2.4. Redundancy and Resilience:

- Implement redundancy in cooling systems, including backup chillers or cooling units, to mitigate the risk of cooling failures.

- Regularly test and maintain cooling equipment to ensure reliable operation.

2.5. Free Cooling and Economizers:

- Explore free cooling methods, such as air-side or water-side economizers, to reduce cooling costs in regions with favorable climates.

- Utilize outside air when conditions permit to reduce reliance on mechanical cooling.

2.6. Contingency Plans:

- Develop contingency plans for cooling failures, including emergency procedures, backup cooling solutions, and pre-defined temperature thresholds for equipment shutdown.

3. Monitoring and Management:

3.1. Environmental Monitoring:

- Implement real-time environmental monitoring solutions to track temperature, humidity, and power consumption.

- Set up alerts and notifications for abnormal conditions to facilitate proactive response.

3.2. Capacity Planning:

- Use historical data and capacity planning tools to anticipate future power and cooling requirements.

- Ensure that expansion plans align with available power and cooling capacity.

3.3. Energy Efficiency Metrics:

- Track key performance indicators (KPIs) related to energy efficiency, such as power usage effectiveness (PUE), to continuously improve data center efficiency.

In conclusion, managing power and cooling requirements is

essential for maintaining the reliability and performance of a data center. By conducting load analyses, designing efficient cooling systems, and implementing monitoring and management solutions, organizations can optimize resource utilization, reduce energy costs, and ensure that their data center remains resilient and responsive to changing IT demands. Power and cooling considerations should be integral to the design and operation of data centers to meet the growing challenges of modern IT infrastructure.

C. Rack Layout and Design in Data Center Setup

The rack layout and design are fundamental aspects of data center setup that directly impact the organization, efficiency, and maintainability of IT infrastructure. An effectively designed rack layout ensures optimal space utilization, efficient cooling, and simplified cable management. In this in-depth exploration, we will delve into the key considerations and best practices for rack layout and design in a data center environment.

1. Rack Selection:

1.1. Standardization: Choose standardized rack sizes, such as 19-inch or 23-inch racks, to ensure compatibility with most IT equipment.

1.2. Rack Capacity: Determine the weight and heat load capacity of each rack to accommodate current and future equipment.

1.3. Rack Features: Consider racks with features like adjustable mounting rails, cable management options, and locking mechanisms for security.

1.4. Rack Location: Plan the placement of racks to optimize airflow, minimize hot spots, and provide easy access for maintenance.

2. Rack Density and Equipment Placement:

2.1. Equipment Placement Strategy: Decide on the arrangement of equipment within racks, such as front-to-back or back-to-front airflow, and adhere to a consistent strategy.

2.2. U-Space Planning: Calculate the number of rack units (U) required for each piece of equipment and plan for future expansion.

2.3. Airflow Considerations: Ensure that equipment placement promotes efficient airflow by positioning hot and cold aisle equipment correctly.

3. Cooling and Ventilation:

3.1. Hot and Cold Aisle Containment: Implement hot and

cold aisle containment solutions to isolate hot and cold airflows, reducing cooling costs and improving efficiency.

3.2. Cable Management: Use vertical and horizontal cable management solutions to keep cables organized and prevent airflow obstructions.

3.3. Rack Ventilation: Select racks with proper ventilation features, such as perforated doors and panels, to facilitate heat dissipation.

3.4. Rack Placement: Avoid placing racks near heat sources or obstructing airflow pathways, and leave sufficient clearance for cooling equipment.

4. Power Distribution:

4.1. Power Distribution Units (PDUs): Install PDUs with appropriate capacity and redundancy to distribute power to equipment within the rack.

4.2. Cable Routing: Ensure that power cables are routed and managed separately from data cables to prevent electromagnetic interference and maintain safety.

4.3. Power Redundancy: Implement power redundancy at the rack level, including dual power supplies for critical equipment.

5. Cable Management:

5.1. Cable Types: Use high-quality, properly rated cables for data and power connections, minimizing the risk of failures or hazards.

5.2. Cable Labeling: Label cables clearly to simplify troubleshooting and maintenance tasks.

5.3. Cable Length: Use appropriate cable lengths to reduce excess slack and maintain a tidy rack layout.

5.4. Cable Paths: Establish cable paths that minimize cable crossings and interference with equipment airflow.

6. Security and Access Control:

6.1. Rack Locking: Secure racks with locking mechanisms to prevent unauthorized access and tampering.

6.2. Access Logging: Implement access control systems that log and track who accesses the racks and when.

6.3. Surveillance: Install surveillance cameras to monitor rack areas for security purposes.

7. Documentation:

7.1. Rack Diagrams: Maintain up-to-date rack diagrams and documentation, including equipment inventory, cable maps, and power distribution layouts.

7.2. Change Management: Implement a change management process to track and document any changes made to rack configurations.

In conclusion, an effective rack layout and design are crucial for optimizing space, airflow, cooling, and cable management in a data center environment. By carefully planning and adhering to best practices, organizations can ensure the reliability, maintainability, and scalability of their IT infrastructure while minimizing the risk of downtime and operational inefficiencies. Rack design should be an integral part of the broader data center strategy to meet the evolving demands of modern IT environments.

D. Server Hardware Setup in Data Center

Server hardware setup is a critical component of data center operations, ensuring that servers are configured, installed, and maintained to meet the performance, reliability, and security requirements of the organization's IT infrastructure. In this in-depth exploration, we will delve into the key considerations and best practices for server hardware setup in a data center environment.

1. Server Selection:

1.1. Purpose and Workload: Choose server hardware that aligns with the specific purpose and workload requirements. Consider factors such as processing power, memory, storage capacity, and network connectivity.

1.2. Scalability: Opt for servers that allow for easy scalability, enabling the addition of resources as demand grows.

1.3. Redundancy: Consider redundancy at the server level by deploying multiple servers in a cluster or configuring redundant components (e.g., power supplies, network adapters) to ensure high availability.

1.4. Compatibility: Ensure that the selected server hardware is compatible with the chosen operating systems and virtualization platforms.

2. Rack Mounting:

2.1. Rails and Mounting Kits: Use appropriate mounting rails and kits to securely install servers in rack enclosures. Ensure that racks can support the weight and dimensions of the servers.

2.2. Airflow: Position servers in the rack to optimize airflow and adhere to hot or cold aisle containment strategies.

2.3. Cable Management: Plan for cable management within

the rack to maintain a tidy and organized setup, preventing cable interference with server components.

3. Hardware Configuration:

3.1. BIOS and Firmware: Update server BIOS and firmware to the latest versions to ensure compatibility, security patches, and performance improvements.

3.2. RAID Configuration: Set up RAID configurations for data redundancy and performance, if applicable.

3.3. Network Configuration: Configure network interfaces, including IP addresses, VLANs, and bonding for redundancy and load balancing.

3.4. Remote Management: Enable remote management interfaces (e.g., IPMI, iDRAC, iLO) for out-of-band server administration and monitoring.

4. Operating System Installation:

4.1. OS Deployment: Install the selected operating system on the servers using standardized deployment methods (e.g., PXE boot, automated scripts, or virtual machine templates).

4.2. Patch Management: Implement a patch management strategy to keep the operating system and software up to date with security and performance updates.

4.3. Configuration Management: Use configuration management tools (e.g., Puppet, Ansible, Chef) to automate and standardize server configurations.

5. Hardware Monitoring:

5.1. Hardware Health Monitoring: Implement hardware monitoring solutions to continuously monitor server components (e.g., CPU, memory, storage, power supplies) for issues and failures.

5.2. Alerts and Notifications: Configure alerts and notifications for critical hardware events to enable rapid response and troubleshooting.

6. Security Measures:

6.1. Physical Security: Secure server hardware against physical threats by using locking racks and access control measures.

6.2. BIOS Security: Enable BIOS security features such as password protection and secure boot to prevent unauthorized access and tampering.

6.3. Firewall and Intrusion Detection: Implement network security measures, including firewalls and intrusion detection systems, to protect servers from external threats.

7. Backup and Recovery:

7.1. Backup Strategy: Develop a backup strategy for server data, including regular backups, off-site storage, and disaster recovery plans.

7.2. Server Imaging: Create server images to expedite recovery and replacement in case of hardware failures.

8. Documentation:

8.1. Asset Inventory: Maintain an up-to-date inventory of all server hardware, including serial numbers, warranty information, and configuration details.

8.2. Configuration Records: Document server configurations, including hardware specifications, software versions, and network settings.

8.3. Change Control: Implement a change control process to track and document any changes made to server hardware and configurations.

In conclusion, effective server hardware setup is crucial for the performance, reliability, and security of data center operations. By adhering to best practices in server selection, rack mounting, hardware configuration, operating system installation, monitoring, security, and documentation, organizations can ensure that their server infrastructure meets the demands of modern IT environments while minimizing risks and downtime. Server hardware setup should be part of a comprehensive data center strategy that focuses on efficiency, scalability, and high availability.

E. Network Infrastructure in Data Center Setup

The network infrastructure is the central nervous system of a data center, responsible for connecting servers, storage, and other devices, enabling communication, and ensuring the efficient flow of data. A well-designed network infrastructure is crucial for the performance, reliability, and security of data center operations. In this in-depth exploration, we will delve into the key considerations and best practices for network infrastructure in a data center environment.

1. Network Architecture:

1.1. Local Area Network (LAN):

- LAN design focuses on connecting devices within the data center. Key considerations include topology (e.g., Ethernet, Fibre Channel), speed (e.g., 1Gbps, 10Gbps, 40Gbps, 100Gbps), and redundancy.

1.2. Wide Area Network (WAN):

- WAN connections link data centers, remote offices, or cloud resources. Network architecture should ensure low latency, high bandwidth, and secure connections.

1.3. Virtual Private Network (VPN):

- VPNs provide secure communication over public networks. Implement VPNs for remote access, site-to-site connections, or secure data transfer.

2. Network Equipment:

2.1. Routers and Switches:

- Select high-performance routers and switches that support the data center's bandwidth requirements. Implement redundancy for critical components.

2.2. Load Balancers:

- Load balancers distribute traffic across multiple servers for load distribution and high availability. Ensure proper configuration and monitoring.

2.3. Firewalls and Intrusion Detection/Prevention Systems (IDS/IPS):

- Implement firewalls and IDS/IPS to protect the network from unauthorized access, attacks, and intrusions.

2.4. Network Appliances:

- Deploy specialized appliances for tasks like content filtering, traffic shaping, and application acceleration.

3. Network Segmentation:

3.1. VLANs (Virtual LANs):

- Use VLANs to logically segment the network, improving security and traffic management.

3.2. Subnetting:

- Subnetting divides IP address ranges into smaller subnetworks, enhancing network efficiency and security.

3.3. DMZ (Demilitarized Zone):

- Implement a DMZ for hosting publicly accessible services, isolating them from the internal network.

4. Redundancy and High Availability:

4.1. Redundant Paths:

- Ensure redundant network paths to prevent single points of failure. Use technologies like Spanning Tree Protocol (STP) or Rapid Spanning Tree Protocol (RSTP) for loop prevention.

4.2. Link Aggregation:

- Use link aggregation (e.g., LACP) to combine multiple network links into a single logical link for increased bandwidth and redundancy.

4.3. Dual Data Centers:

- For mission-critical applications, consider dual data center configurations with geographical redundancy.

5. Quality of Service (QoS):

5.1. Traffic Prioritization:

- Implement QoS policies to prioritize critical traffic (e.g., voice, video) and ensure a consistent user experience.

5.2. Bandwidth Management:

- Use QoS to manage bandwidth allocation, preventing one type of traffic from overwhelming the network.

6. Monitoring and Management:

6.1. Network Monitoring Tools:

- Utilize network monitoring tools to track network performance, detect anomalies, and troubleshoot issues.

6.2. Configuration Management:

- Implement configuration management for network devices to maintain consistency and manage changes effectively.

6.3. Network Automation:

- Leverage automation tools to streamline network provisioning, configuration, and management.

7. Security Measures:

7.1. Access Control:

- Implement strong access control measures, including user authentication and authorization, to restrict network access.

7.2. Network Security Policies:

- Define and enforce network security policies, including firewall rules, intrusion detection, and encryption.

7.3. Regular Security Audits:

- Conduct regular security audits and penetration testing to identify vulnerabilities and weaknesses in the network.

8. Scalability:

8.1. Scalable Design:

- Plan for network scalability to accommodate future growth in data center operations.

8.2. Cloud Integration:

- Consider integrating with cloud services for scalability and hybrid cloud deployments.

In conclusion, a well-designed and managed network infrastructure is essential for the success of a data center. By considering network architecture, equipment selection, redundancy, segmentation, quality of service, monitoring, security measures, and scalability, organizations can ensure that their network meets the demands of modern data center environments while providing the performance, reliability, and security required for critical operations. Network infrastructure should be a central focus in data center planning and ongoing management.

F. Cabling and Cable Management in Data Center Setup

Cabling and cable management are integral aspects of data center design and maintenance, ensuring that data flows efficiently, reliably, and without interruptions between servers, networking equipment, and other critical infrastructure components. Effective cable management not only enhances the organization and aesthetics of the data center but also contributes to improved airflow, easier maintenance, and reduced downtime. In this in-depth exploration, we will delve into the key considerations and best practices for cabling and cable management in a data center environment.

1. Cable Types and Selection:

1.1. Ethernet Cabling:

- Use high-quality Ethernet cables (e.g., Cat 6, Cat 6a, Cat 7) for data connectivity between servers, switches, and routers.

- Consider fiber optic cables (single-mode or multi-mode) for high-speed, long-distance connections.

1.2. Power Cabling:

- Choose appropriate power cables for connecting servers, power distribution units (PDUs), and uninterruptible power supplies (UPS).

- Ensure cables are rated for the current load and are of the correct gauge (AWG) to prevent overheating.

1.3. Cable Length:

- Select cable lengths that minimize excess slack while allowing flexibility for equipment adjustments and maintenance.

1.4. Color Coding:

- Use color-coded cables to differentiate between data, power, and management connections.

- Follow industry standards for cable color coding to simplify troubleshooting.

2. Cable Routing and Organization:

2.1. Horizontal and Vertical Cable Management:

- Implement both horizontal and vertical cable management solutions to guide and secure cables within racks and enclosures.

2.2. Cable Trays and Ladders:

- Install cable trays or ladders above racks to route and support cables, keeping them organized and preventing cable sag.

2.3. Cable Labels and Markers:

- Label cables at both ends with clear, standardized labels or markers that include information about their source and destination.

2.4. Velcro Straps and Cable Ties:

- Use Velcro straps or reusable cable ties for bundling cables, as they are easier to adjust and remove than single-use plastic ties.

2.5. Cable Management Arms and Rings:

- Deploy cable management arms and rings within racks to guide and secure cables, preventing tangles and obstructions.

3. Cable Pathways:

3.1. Aisle Containment:

- Implement hot and cold aisle containment strategies to separate airflow and cable pathways, reducing the risk of heat-related issues.

3.2. Overhead and Underfloor Pathways:

- Plan cable pathways both above and below the raised floor to accommodate network, power, and cooling cables.

3.3. Avoiding Cable Crossings:

- Minimize cable crossings, which can lead to interference and make it difficult to trace and manage cables.

4. Cable Testing and Certification:

4.1. Cable Testing:

- Conduct cable testing (e.g., cable continuity, signal quality) during installation to ensure proper functionality.

4.2. Certification:

- Consider certifying cables using tools such as a cable certifier or verifier to verify compliance with industry standards.

5. Redundancy and Documentation:

5.1. Redundant Paths:

- Implement redundant cable paths for critical connections to ensure high availability.

- Document the redundancy configurations for quick reference during troubleshooting.

5.2. Cable Documentation:

- Maintain comprehensive cable documentation, including cable inventories, connection diagrams, and cable routing plans.

6. Regular Audits and Maintenance:

6.1. Periodic Audits:

- Conduct regular audits of cable installations to identify and address issues like damaged cables or connections.

6.2. Cable Management Software:

- Utilize cable management software solutions to track and manage cables, making it easier to locate and manage cables within the data center.

7. Safety Measures:

7.1. Cable Clearance:

- Ensure that cables do not obstruct airflow pathways, emergency exits, or access to equipment.

7.2. Cable Labeling:

- Clearly label power cables to indicate voltage and the associated equipment to prevent electrical mishaps.

In conclusion, effective cabling and cable management are essential for maintaining a well-organized, reliable, and efficient data center. By adhering to best practices in cable selection, routing, organization, testing, redundancy, and documentation, organizations can reduce the risk of downtime, simplify troubleshooting, and ensure that their data center infrastructure meets the demands of modern IT environments. Proper cable management should be a core component of data center planning and ongoing maintenance.

G. Storage Solutions in Data Center Setup

Storage solutions are a critical component of data center infrastructure, responsible for storing and managing the vast amounts of data generated by organizations. Effective storage design and management are essential for ensuring data availability, scalability, and performance. In this in-depth exploration, we will delve into the key considerations and best practices for storage solutions in a data center environment.

1. Types of Storage Technologies:

1.1. SAN (Storage Area Network):

- SANs are dedicated high-speed networks that connect servers to shared storage devices. They are ideal for high-performance applications and provide features like block-level access and redundancy.

1.2. NAS (Network-Attached Storage):

- NAS devices are file-level storage solutions that use standard network protocols (e.g., NFS, SMB) to provide file shares to network clients. They are suitable for file storage and sharing.

1.3. Object Storage:

- Object storage systems, like Amazon S3 or Azure Blob Storage, are designed for managing vast amounts of unstructured data, including multimedia and backups.

1.4. DAS (Direct-Attached Storage):

- DAS connects storage directly to a single server or a group of servers. While less scalable, DAS can be cost-effective for smaller data centers or specific use cases.

2. Storage Redundancy and High Availability:

2.1. RAID (Redundant Array of Independent Disks):

- Implement RAID configurations to provide data redundancy and improve read/write performance. Common RAID levels include RAID 0, 1, 5, 6, 10, and 50.

2.2. Clustering and Failover:

- Use clustering and failover mechanisms to ensure high availability of storage resources. This involves redundant storage controllers and automated failover in case of hardware or software failures.

2.3. Data Replication:

- Implement data replication solutions to create duplicate copies of data in geographically distant locations for disaster recovery and fault tolerance.

3. Scalability:

3.1. Scalable Architectures:

- Choose storage solutions that support scalable architectures, enabling you to add storage capacity and performance as needed.

3.2. Storage Virtualization:

- Implement storage virtualization to abstract physical storage resources, making them easier to manage and scale.

3.3. Cloud Storage Integration:

- Leverage cloud storage services for scalability and cost-effective storage solutions.

4. Storage Tiering:

4.1. Hot and Cold Data:

- Implement storage tiering to separate frequently accessed (hot) data from infrequently accessed (cold) data. Use high-performance storage for hot data and cost-effective solutions for cold data.

5. Data Backup and Recovery:

5.1. Backup Strategies:

- Develop comprehensive backup strategies, including regular backups, incremental backups, and full backups, to ensure data recoverability in case of data loss or disasters.

5.2. Backup Testing:

- Regularly test backup and recovery procedures to verify their effectiveness.

6. Data Lifecycle Management:

6.1. Data Retention Policies:

- Establish data retention policies that define how long data should be stored and when it should be deleted.

6.2. Archiving:

- Implement data archiving solutions to store historical or regulatory data separately from active data.

7. Performance Optimization:

7.1. Monitoring and Tuning:

- Continuously monitor storage performance and tune configurations as needed to ensure optimal performance for critical applications.

7.2. SSDs (Solid-State Drives):

- Consider using SSDs for high-performance storage needs, as they offer significantly faster data access compared to traditional HDDs.

8. Security Measures:

8.1. Access Control:

- Implement strict access control measures to prevent unauthorized access to storage resources.

8.2. Encryption:

- Encrypt data at rest and in transit to protect sensitive information.

9. Disaster Recovery Planning:

9.1. Disaster Recovery Plans:

- Develop comprehensive disaster recovery plans that include storage recovery procedures and data replication strategies.

9.2. Testing and Drills:

- Regularly test disaster recovery plans through simulated drills and scenarios.

In conclusion, storage solutions are vital for managing data in a data center, and their design and management should align with an organization's data access, redundancy, scalability, and security requirements. By adhering to best practices in storage technology selection, redundancy, scalability, backup and recovery, data lifecycle management, performance optimization, security measures, and disaster recovery planning, organizations can ensure that their storage infrastructure meets the demands of modern data center environments while safeguarding data integrity and availability. Proper storage planning and management are key components of data center success.

H. Redundancy and High Availability in Data Center Setup

Redundancy and high availability are critical aspects of data center design aimed at ensuring that IT services and infrastructure remain operational even in the face of hardware failures, maintenance, or unexpected disruptions. These strategies are essential for minimizing downtime, meeting service-level agreements (SLAs), and delivering a reliable and responsive IT environment. In this in-depth exploration, we will delve into the key considerations and best practices for redundancy and high availability in a data center environment.

1. Hardware Redundancy:

1.1. Power Redundancy:

- Implement redundant power supplies and power distribution units (PDUs) to ensure uninterrupted power delivery to critical equipment.

- Use uninterruptible power supplies (UPS) and backup generators to maintain power during outages.

1.2. Network Redundancy:

- Utilize multiple network paths and network devices (routers, switches) to prevent network failures from causing downtime.

- Implement technologies like Spanning Tree Protocol (STP) or Virtual Router Redundancy Protocol (VRRP) for network path redundancy.

1.3. Server and Storage Redundancy:

- Deploy redundant servers and storage systems to maintain service availability.

- Use clustering and load balancing to distribute workloads across redundant servers.

1.4. Cooling Redundancy:

- Ensure redundancy in cooling systems to prevent overheating and maintain a consistent temperature within the data center.

2. Data Center Layout:

2.1. Hot and Cold Aisles:

- Organize data center racks into hot and cold aisles to isolate hot air exhaust from cold air intake, improving cooling efficiency.

2.2. Fire Suppression and Environmental Controls:

- Implement fire suppression systems and environmental controls to protect equipment and maintain optimal conditions.

3. Data Replication:

3.1. Synchronous and Asynchronous Replication:

- Use synchronous replication for real-time redundancy, ensuring data consistency between primary and secondary sites.

- Asynchronous replication provides flexibility by replicating data at scheduled intervals but may have a slight lag.

3.2. Geographical Redundancy:

- Establish redundant data centers in geographically distant locations to protect against regional disasters.

4. Load Balancing:

4.1. Application Load Balancers (ALB):

- Implement ALBs to distribute traffic across multiple servers or data centers, ensuring even workloads and high availability.

4.2. Global Server Load Balancing (GSLB):

- Use GSLB to distribute traffic across multiple data centers in different locations, providing geographic redundancy.

5. Failover and Switchover Procedures:

5.1. Automatic Failover:

- Set up automated failover mechanisms that detect failures and switch to redundant components without manual intervention.

5.2. Manual Switchover:

- Prepare documented procedures for manual switchover in case of planned maintenance or complex failure scenarios.

6. Testing and Simulations:

6.1. Failover Testing:

- Regularly test failover procedures and redundancy configurations to validate their effectiveness.

6.2. Disaster Recovery Drills:

- Conduct disaster recovery drills to ensure data center operations can be resumed swiftly in case of catastrophic events.

7. Monitoring and Alerts:

7.1. Continuous Monitoring:

- Implement real-time monitoring of critical infrastructure components to detect anomalies and failures promptly.

7.2. Alerting Systems:

- Set up alerting systems that notify administrators and operators when failures or issues occur.

8. Documentation:

8.1. Redundancy Plans:

- Document redundancy plans, including network diagrams, failover procedures, and contact information for key personnel.

8.2. Change Control:

- Establish change control processes to ensure that any modifications to the data center environment are well-documented and do not compromise redundancy.

In conclusion, redundancy and high availability are paramount in maintaining a resilient and responsive data center. By carefully considering hardware redundancy, data replication, load balancing, failover procedures, testing, monitoring, and documentation, organizations can ensure that their data center infrastructure meets the demands of modern IT environments while minimizing downtime and maximizing service reliability. Redundancy and high availability planning should be an integral part of data center design and ongoing management.

I. Data Center Operations: Ensuring Efficient and Reliable Infrastructure Management

Data center operations encompass the day-to-day activities, processes, and procedures required to ensure the efficient, secure, and reliable functioning of a data center. Effective data center operations are essential for delivering high-performance IT services, minimizing downtime, and meeting the demands of modern organizations. In this in-depth exploration, we will delve into the key considerations and best practices for data center operations.

1. Facility Management:

1.1. Physical Security:

- Implement strict access control measures, surveillance systems, and biometric authentication to safeguard data center premises.

1.2. Environmental Controls:

- Monitor and control temperature, humidity, and airflow to maintain optimal conditions for equipment.

1.3. Fire Suppression:

- Install fire detection and suppression systems to protect against fire hazards without damaging sensitive equipment.

1.4. Power Management:

- Ensure reliable and uninterrupted power supply through redundant power feeds, uninterruptible power supplies (UPS), and backup generators.

1.5. Rack Layout and Organization:

- Arrange racks and equipment for optimal airflow, cable management, and easy access for maintenance.

2. Asset Management:

2.1. Inventory Management:

- Maintain an up-to-date inventory of all data center assets, including servers, storage devices, networking equipment, and software licenses.

2.2. Asset Tracking:

- Use asset tracking systems to monitor the location, status, and configuration of assets throughout their lifecycle.

2.3. Decommissioning:

- Develop procedures for retiring and decommissioning outdated or underutilized equipment, ensuring proper data erasure and disposal.

3. Change Management:

3.1. Change Control Procedures:

- Establish change control processes to document and authorize any modifications or updates to the data center environment.

3.2. Testing and Validation:

- Prioritize thorough testing and validation of changes to assess their impact on data center operations.

3.3. Rollback Plans:

- Develop rollback plans in case changes result in unexpected issues or failures.

4. Monitoring and Alerting:

4.1. Real-time Monitoring:

- Implement comprehensive monitoring solutions that track the performance, health, and status of all data center components.

4.2. Alerts and Notifications:

- Configure alerting systems to provide timely notifications for critical events, enabling rapid response to issues.

4.3. Predictive Analytics:

- Utilize predictive analytics to identify potential problems before they impact data center operations, allowing for proactive intervention.

5. Security Measures:

5.1. Access Control:

- Enforce strict access control measures, including multi-factor authentication and role-based access, to prevent unauthorized access.

5.2. Intrusion Detection:

- Deploy intrusion detection systems (IDS) and intrusion prevention systems (IPS) to monitor and protect against security threats.

5.3. Regular Audits:

- Conduct security audits and vulnerability assessments to identify and mitigate potential risks.

6. Disaster Recovery and Business Continuity:

6.1. Disaster Recovery Plans:

- Develop comprehensive disaster recovery plans that define how data center operations can be resumed swiftly in case of catastrophic events.

6.2. Backup Strategies:

- Establish robust backup strategies that ensure data recoverability in case of data loss or disasters.

7. Incident Management:

7.1. Incident Response Plans:

- Create incident response plans to address various types of incidents, from hardware failures to security breaches.

7.2. Documentation:

- Thoroughly document incidents, responses, and resolutions to facilitate post-incident analysis and process improvement.

8. Training and Skills Development:

8.1. Personnel Training:

- Invest in ongoing training and certification programs to ensure data center staff have the skills and knowledge needed to manage complex infrastructure.

8.2. Cross-Training:

- Cross-train personnel to ensure redundancy in skillsets and reduce reliance on individual experts.

In conclusion, effective data center operations are essential for maintaining a robust and responsive IT infrastructure. By focusing on facility management, asset management, change control, monitoring, security measures, disaster recovery, incident management, and personnel training, organizations can ensure that their data center operates efficiently and reliably, meeting the demands of modern IT environments while minimizing risks and downtime. Data center operations should be an ongoing focus to adapt to changing technology and business requirements.

J. Security Measures in Data Center Operations

Security is a paramount concern in data center operations, as data centers house critical infrastructure and sensitive information. Implementing robust security measures is essential to protect against threats, breaches, and unauthorized access. In this in-depth exploration, we will delve into the key considerations and best practices for security measures in data center operations.

1. Physical Security:

1.1. Access Control:

- Implement stringent access control measures, including biometric authentication, card readers, and access logs, to restrict entry to authorized personnel only.

1.2. Surveillance Systems:

- Deploy surveillance cameras throughout the data center facility to monitor and record activities, enhancing physical security.

1.3. Intrusion Detection:

- Install intrusion detection systems (IDS) and alarms to detect unauthorized physical access and tampering with equipment or infrastructure.

1.4. Mantraps and Turnstiles:

- Use mantraps and turnstiles at entrances to ensure only one person enters at a time and to prevent tailgating.

1.5. Secure Racks and Cabinets:

- Secure racks and cabinets with locks and monitoring systems to protect against unauthorized access to servers and networking equipment.

2. Network Security:

2.1. Firewall Protection:

- Deploy firewalls to filter incoming and outgoing network traffic, allowing only authorized traffic to enter or leave the data center.

2.2. Intrusion Detection and Prevention:

- Utilize intrusion detection systems (IDS) and intrusion prevention systems (IPS) to monitor network traffic for suspicious activity and block threats.

2.3. Network Segmentation:

- Implement network segmentation to isolate sensitive data and critical infrastructure from less secure areas, reducing the attack surface.

2.4. Virtual LANs (VLANs):

- Use VLANs to logically separate network segments, enhancing security by isolating traffic.

2.5. Encryption:

- Encrypt data in transit and at rest to protect it from eavesdropping or theft.

3. Data Security:

3.1. Data Encryption:

- Implement encryption for data at rest and data in transit, including sensitive databases and backups.

3.2. Data Classification:

- Classify data based on sensitivity and apply access controls and encryption accordingly.

3.3. Data Backup and Recovery:

- Ensure that data backups are securely stored and encrypted to prevent unauthorized access to sensitive information.

3.4. Secure Disposal:

- Develop procedures for securely disposing of data storage devices and media to prevent data leaks.

4. Server and Endpoint Security:

4.1. Patch Management:

- Establish patch management processes to keep servers and endpoints up to date with the latest security patches.

4.2. Antivirus and Anti-Malware:

- Install and regularly update antivirus and anti-malware software on servers and endpoints to protect against malicious software.

4.3. Application Security:

- Conduct regular security assessments and code reviews to identify and mitigate vulnerabilities in applications.

5. Security Policies and Procedures:

5.1. Security Policies:

- Develop comprehensive security policies that define security controls, procedures, and guidelines for data center operations.

5.2. Incident Response Plan:

- Create an incident response plan that outlines the steps to follow in case of a security incident, including containment, analysis, and recovery.

5.3. Employee Training:

- Provide security awareness training to all data center staff to educate them about security threats and best practices.

6. Third-Party Audits and Penetration Testing:

6.1. Regular Audits:

- Conduct regular security audits and vulnerability assessments to identify and remediate potential risks.

6.2. Penetration Testing:

- Engage in penetration testing exercises to simulate attacks and test the resilience of security measures.

7. Compliance and Regulatory Standards:

7.1. Compliance Frameworks:

- Ensure that data center operations adhere to industry-specific compliance frameworks and regulatory standards.

7.2. Auditing and Documentation:

- Maintain documentation and auditing records to demonstrate compliance with security standards.

In conclusion, security measures are paramount in data center operations to protect against threats and ensure the confidentiality, integrity, and availability of data and infrastructure. By implementing physical security measures, network security controls, data security practices, server and endpoint security, security policies and procedures, employee training, third-party audits, and compliance with regulatory standards, organizations can fortify their data center operations and minimize the risk of security breaches and incidents. Data center security should be an ongoing focus to adapt to evolving threats and maintain a strong defense posture.

K. Scalability and Growth in Data Center Operations

Scalability and growth are fundamental considerations in data center operations, as organizations constantly adapt to changing business needs, technology advancements, and increasing data demands. Ensuring that a data center can scale efficiently while maintaining optimal performance is crucial for meeting these challenges. In this in-depth exploration, we will delve into the key considerations and best practices for scalability and growth in data center operations.

1. Capacity Planning:

1.1. Forecasting Demand:

- Accurately predict future IT resource requirements, including computing power, storage, and network capacity, based on business growth and data trends.

1.2. Resource Monitoring:

- Continuously monitor the utilization of resources within the data center to identify capacity constraints and bottlenecks.

1.3. Scalability Metrics:

- Define key performance indicators (KPIs) to measure the efficiency and effectiveness of resource scaling efforts.

2. Scalable Architecture:

2.1. Modular Design:

- Adopt a modular data center design that allows for the incremental addition of resources as needed.

2.2. Redundancy and Load Balancing:

- Implement redundancy and load balancing at various levels of the infrastructure to distribute workloads and ensure high availability.

2.3. Converged and Hyper-Converged Infrastructure:

- Consider converged and hyper-converged infrastructure solutions that simplify resource scaling by integrating compute, storage, and networking components.

2.4. Cloud Integration:

- Leverage cloud services to extend data center resources when needed, adopting a hybrid cloud or multi-cloud strategy for scalability.

3. Infrastructure as Code (IaC):

3.1. Automation:

- Embrace IaC principles to automate the provisioning and management of infrastructure resources, allowing for rapid and consistent scaling.

3.2. Infrastructure Templates:

- Use infrastructure templates (e.g., Terraform, AWS CloudFormation) to define and provision resources programmatically.

3.3. Version Control:

- Employ version control systems (e.g., Git) to manage and track changes to infrastructure code, ensuring reproducibility and accountability.

4. Network Scalability:

4.1. Scalable Network Architecture:

- Design a scalable network architecture that accommodates

increasing data traffic, adding switches, routers, and access points as necessary.

4.2. Software-Defined Networking (SDN):

- Implement SDN technologies to dynamically adjust network configurations and resources based on demand.

4.3. Quality of Service (QoS):

- Prioritize network traffic through QoS policies to ensure critical applications receive adequate bandwidth during periods of high demand.

5. Storage Scalability:

5.1. Storage Tiering:

- Employ storage tiering to optimize resource allocation, moving frequently accessed data to high-performance storage and less-accessed data to cost-effective storage.

5.2. Scale-Out Storage:

- Choose scale-out storage solutions that allow for the addition of storage nodes as data capacity requirements increase.

5.3. Object Storage:

- Consider object storage systems that can seamlessly scale to accommodate large volumes of unstructured data.

6. Cooling and Power:

6.1. Cooling Efficiency:

- Optimize cooling systems to accommodate increased heat loads efficiently, utilizing techniques like hot/cold aisle containment.

6.2. Power Distribution:

- Ensure that power distribution can handle additional loads, considering power redundancy and backup generators for uninterrupted service.

7. Documentation and Asset Management:

7.1. Updated Documentation:

- Maintain up-to-date documentation of all hardware, software, and infrastructure configurations to support efficient scaling and troubleshooting.

7.2. Asset Inventory:

- Track and manage inventory to ensure that resources can be easily identified and allocated as needed.

8. Testing and Validation:

8.1. Scalability Testing:

- Conduct scalability testing to evaluate how well the data center infrastructure can handle increased loads and identify any performance bottlenecks.

8.2. Disaster Recovery Testing:

- Include scalability considerations in disaster recovery testing to ensure that resources can be scaled up in a recovery scenario.

In conclusion, scalability and growth in data center operations are essential for adapting to changing business and technology landscapes. By incorporating capacity planning, scalable architecture design, infrastructure as code principles, network and storage scalability, efficient cooling and power management, robust documentation and asset management, and comprehensive testing and validation, organizations can ensure that their data center operations can flexibly and efficiently meet increased demands while maintaining optimal performance and reliability. Scalability should be a core consideration in data center planning and ongoing management to support future growth and adaptability.

L. Documentation and Asset Management in Data Center Operations

Documentation and asset management are foundational aspects of data center operations. A well-organized and up-to-date documentation system, combined with effective asset management, ensures that a data center runs efficiently, securely, and with minimal downtime. In this in-depth exploration, we will delve into the key considerations and best practices for documentation and asset management in data center operations.

1. Documentation Practices:

1.1. Infrastructure Inventory:

- Maintain a comprehensive inventory of all data center assets, including servers, networking equipment, storage devices, and power and cooling systems.

1.2. Configuration Records:

- Document the configuration details of each asset, including hardware specifications, firmware versions, software versions, and network settings.

1.3. Network Topology Diagrams:

- Create network topology diagrams that illustrate the physical and logical layout of the data center, including the connectivity of devices and network segments.

1.4. Rack Layouts:

- Develop rack layouts that depict the placement of servers, switches, and other equipment within data center racks, ensuring efficient use of space and airflow.

1.5. Cable Management:

- Maintain records of cable connections, including patch panel assignments, cable types, and cable routes, to facilitate troubleshooting and changes.

1.6. Security Policies:

- Document security policies and access controls, including who has access to the data center and under what conditions.

2. Change Management:

2.1. Change Documentation:

- Record all changes made to the data center environment, including hardware upgrades, software updates, and network configuration changes.

2.2. Change Authorization:

- Implement a change control process that requires proper authorization and documentation before any changes are executed.

2.3. Rollback Plans:

- Develop rollback plans for changes to enable a quick return to the previous state in case of unexpected issues or failures.

3. Disaster Recovery Plans:

3.1. DR Documentation:

- Create and regularly update detailed disaster recovery plans that outline recovery procedures, including asset recovery and data restoration processes.

3.2. Backup and Restore Procedures:

- Document backup and restore procedures, including backup schedules, retention policies, and recovery point objectives.

4. Security Documentation:

4.1. Security Policies:

- Document security policies, procedures, and controls, including access control lists, firewall rules, and intrusion detection configurations.

4.2. Incident Response Plans:

- Maintain incident response plans that outline procedures for identifying, reporting, and mitigating security incidents.

5. Asset Management:

5.1. Asset Identification:

- Assign unique identifiers (e.g., asset tags, barcodes) to all data center assets to facilitate tracking and management.

5.2. Asset Tracking:

- Implement asset tracking systems and databases to record asset details, including purchase date, warranty information, and maintenance history.

5.3. Lifecycle Management:

- Track the entire lifecycle of assets, from procurement to decommissioning, to ensure efficient resource utilization.

5.4. Maintenance Scheduling:

- Schedule regular maintenance and servicing of assets, documenting maintenance activities and results.

6. Training and Access Control:

6.1. Employee Training:

- Provide training to data center personnel on proper documentation practices and the use of asset management systems.

6.2. Access Control:

- Implement access controls to restrict access to documentation and asset management systems to authorized personnel only.

7. Documentation Tools:

7.1. Document Management Systems:

- Utilize document management systems and databases to organize and store documentation securely.

7.2. Asset Tracking Software:

- Employ asset tracking software to maintain accurate records of asset details and locations.

7.3. Version Control:

- Implement version control systems for documentation to track changes and revisions over time.

In conclusion, effective documentation and asset management are essential for the smooth and secure operation of a data center. By adopting best practices in documentation, change management, disaster recovery planning, security documentation, asset identification, tracking, and lifecycle management, organizations can ensure that their data center operations are well-documented, organized, and capable of responding to changes and challenges with efficiency and reliability. Documentation and asset management should be an ongoing focus in data center operations to support resource optimization and minimize risks.

CHAPTER 7

Cabling, Crimping, and Hardware Installation

Cabling, crimping, and hardware installation are foundational aspects of data center operations and IT infrastructure management. These essential processes lay the groundwork for establishing a reliable and efficient IT environment. In this introductory overview, we will explore the significance of cabling, crimping, and hardware installation in modern organizations and the critical role they play in ensuring seamless connectivity, data transmission, and hardware functionality within a data center or IT infrastructure setting.

Efficient cabling and crimping techniques, alongside meticulous hardware installation procedures, are vital components in establishing a robust IT infrastructure. They determine the quality of network connections, the speed of data transfer, and the overall reliability of hardware components. Proper cabling and crimping ensure that data flows smoothly through a network, while expert hardware installation guarantees the stability and optimal performance of servers, networking devices, and storage systems.

In the following sections, we will delve into these areas in greater detail, exploring the various types of cabling, crimping methods, and hardware components commonly encountered in IT infrastructure management. We will also examine best practices, tools, and technologies associated with each domain, offering insights into how organizations can achieve the highest level of connectivity, data integrity, and hardware functionality while maintaining the utmost precision and reliability in their IT operations.

A. Types of Cabling in IT Infrastructure: Ethernet, Fiber Optic, and More

Cabling is the backbone of IT infrastructure, providing the physical connections that enable data transmission within and between devices. Choosing the right type of cabling is crucial to ensure optimal performance, bandwidth, and reliability. In this in-depth exploration, we will delve into the primary types of cabling used in IT infrastructure, with a focus on Ethernet and fiber optic cables, and their applications, advantages, and considerations.

1. Ethernet Cabling:

Ethernet cables are widely used for local area network (LAN) connections within data centers, offices, and homes. They come in various categories, each offering different performance levels and capabilities:

1.1. Cat 5e (Category 5e):

- Cat 5e cables support data rates of up to 1 Gbps (Gigabit per second) and are suitable for most standard Ethernet connections.

- They are commonly used for connecting computers, printers, and other devices in office environments.

1.2. Cat 6 (Category 6):

- Cat 6 cables provide higher performance, supporting data rates of up to 10 Gbps.

- They are ideal for high-speed LANs, data centers, and environments where reliable and high-bandwidth connections are essential.

1.3. Cat 6a (Category 6a):

- Cat 6a cables offer even greater performance, supporting 10 Gbps over longer distances and with reduced crosstalk.

- They are often used in data center backbones and other high-performance networking scenarios.

1.4. Cat 7 (Category 7):

- Cat 7 cables provide exceptional performance, with support for data rates up to 10 Gbps over longer distances.

- They are shielded to minimize interference and are suitable for demanding applications like 4K video streaming.

2. Fiber Optic Cabling:

Fiber optic cables use light signals to transmit data, making them highly efficient for long-distance and high-bandwidth applications. They come in several types:

2.1. Single-Mode Fiber (SMF):

- SMF cables are designed for long-distance transmission and offer the highest bandwidth capabilities.

- They are commonly used for interconnecting data centers, long-haul telecommunications, and high-speed internet backbones.

2.2. Multi-Mode Fiber (MMF):

- MMF cables are suitable for shorter distances and offer lower bandwidth compared to SMF.

- They are commonly used for campus networks, LAN connections, and backbone links within data centers.

3. Coaxial Cabling:

Coaxial cables consist of a central conductor surrounded by insulation, a metallic shield, and an outer insulating layer. They are commonly used for cable television (CATV) and some data transmission applications. Types of coaxial cables include RG-6 and RG-59.

4. Twisted Pair Cabling:

Twisted pair cables, like Ethernet cables, consist of pairs of insulated copper wires twisted together. They are widely used for voice and data communications. In addition to Ethernet cables, they include telephone cables and various types of audio and video cables.

5. USB Cabling:

Universal Serial Bus (USB) cables are used for connecting a wide range of peripherals and devices, including printers, external hard drives, and smartphones, to computers and other host devices.

6. HDMI Cabling:

High-Definition Multimedia Interface (HDMI) cables are used for transmitting high-quality audio and video signals, making them essential for connecting devices like televisions, monitors, and gaming consoles.

7. Power Cabling:

Power cables are used to supply electrical power to various IT infrastructure components, including servers, networking equipment, and data center infrastructure.

Considerations for Choosing Cabling:

- **Bandwidth Requirements:** Determine the data transfer speed and bandwidth needed for your specific application.

- **Distance:** Consider the distance over which data needs to be transmitted, as this can affect the choice of cabling.

- **Interference:** Evaluate potential sources of electromagnetic interference and select shielded cables when necessary.

- **Future-Proofing:** Choose cabling that can accommodate future technology upgrades to avoid frequent replacements.

- **Cost:** Assess the cost-effectiveness of different cable types in relation to your specific needs.

- **Environmental Factors:** Consider factors like temperature, humidity, and exposure to elements when selecting cabling for outdoor or harsh environments.

In conclusion, selecting the right type of cabling is a critical decision in IT infrastructure planning. Ethernet and fiber optic cables are among the most commonly used and offer different performance characteristics to suit various applications. It's essential to carefully assess your specific requirements, budget constraints, and environmental conditions to make informed choices that ensure reliable and efficient data transmission within your IT infrastructure.

B. Cable Routing and Organization in IT Infrastructure

Cable routing and organization are essential aspects of IT infrastructure management, particularly in data centers and network environments. Proper cable management not only improves the aesthetics of the infrastructure but also enhances performance, reduces downtime, and simplifies troubleshooting. In this in-depth exploration, we will delve into the significance of cable routing and organization, best practices, and techniques to ensure a clean and efficient cabling infrastructure.

Significance of Cable Routing and Organization:

1. **Improved Airflow and Cooling:** Organized cables enable efficient airflow within racks and enclosures, preventing overheating and ensuring equipment operates optimally.

2. **Ease of Maintenance:** Well-organized cables make it easier to identify and access specific connections, reducing the time and effort required for maintenance, upgrades, and troubleshooting.

3. **Reduced Downtime:** Neatly routed cables minimize the risk

of accidental disconnections or damage, which can lead to costly downtime.

4. **Enhanced Aesthetics:** A tidy and organized cabling infrastructure improves the overall appearance of data center or network cabinets, making it easier to manage and maintain.

Best Practices for Cable Routing and Organization:

1. **Use Cable Management Hardware:**

   - Employ cable management accessories such as cable trays, cable managers, and raceways to route and secure cables effectively.

2. **Label Cables:**

   - Label both ends of each cable with clear and unique identifiers to simplify tracing and identification.

3. **Color Coding:**

   - Use color-coded cables or cable ties to distinguish between different types of connections (e.g., data, power) or network segments.

4. **Plan Cable Routes:**

   - Design cable routes that minimize crossover and interference while ensuring that cables are not tightly bent or kinked.

5. **Separate Power and Data Cables:**

   - Keep power cables separate from data cables to reduce electromagnetic interference (EMI) and maintain signal integrity.

6. **Maintain Slack Loops:**

   - Leave slack loops in cables to allow for equipment movement and reduce strain on connectors.

7. **Velcro or Hook-and-Loop Ties:**

   - Use Velcro or hook-and-loop cable ties instead of zip ties for easy reusability and adjustments.

8. **Cable Management Documentation:**

   - Create documentation that includes cable routing diagrams and labeling schemes for future reference.

9. **Regular Audits:**

   - Conduct regular cable audits to identify and remove unused or obsolete cables, keeping the infrastructure clutter-free.

10. Secure Cables at Entry/Exit Points:

- Secure cables at entry and exit points of racks or cabinets to prevent accidental disconnections.

11. Implement Cable Management Channels:

- Use cable management channels within rack enclosures to guide cables from one side to the other.

12. Top-Down Cable Routing:

- Route cables from the top of the rack or cabinet down to the equipment to minimize cable congestion.

13. Use Patch Panels:

- Deploy patch panels for network connections, consolidating and organizing multiple cable terminations in one location.

14. Properly Train Staff:

- Train data center and IT personnel in cable management best practices to ensure consistency and adherence to standards.

Techniques for Specific Cable Types:

- **Fiber Optic Cables:**

    - Fiber optic cables should be carefully bent to avoid excessive stress on the cable. Use appropriate bend radius guidelines.

- **Power Cables:**

    - Keep power cables separate from data cables to minimize EMI. Use dedicated power distribution units (PDUs) to manage power cables.

- **Ethernet Cables:**

    - Use cable management panels and cable ties to neatly organize Ethernet cables, keeping them free from tangles and snags.

- **Large Bundles of Cables:**

    - For large bundles of cables, consider cable lacing or spiral wrap to maintain organization and ease of maintenance.

In conclusion, cable routing and organization are critical for maintaining a well-functioning IT infrastructure. Employing best practices, utilizing cable management hardware, labeling cables, and training staff to adhere to these guidelines will result in a cleaner, more efficient, and easier-to-maintain cabling infrastructure. A properly organized cable infrastructure not only enhances performance but also contributes to the overall reliability and aesthetics of the data center or network environment.

C. Crimping and Termination Techniques in IT Infrastructure

Crimping and termination techniques are essential skills in IT infrastructure management, particularly in networking and cabling systems. These techniques involve attaching connectors to the ends of cables, ensuring reliable and secure connections for data transmission. In this in-depth exploration, we will delve into crimping and termination techniques, the tools involved, and best practices for achieving quality terminations in Ethernet and other cabling systems.

Crimping and Termination Basics:

1. **Purpose of Crimping and Termination:**

   - Crimping and termination are used to attach connectors to the ends of cables, allowing for the connection of devices and equipment within IT infrastructure.

2. **Common Connector Types:**

- The choice of connector type depends on the application. Common connectors include RJ-45 (Ethernet), RJ-11 (telephone), BNC (coaxial), and SC/ST/LC (fiber optic).

Tools and Equipment:

1. **Crimping Tool:**

- A crimping tool is essential for attaching connectors to cables. It compresses the connector onto the cable, creating a secure connection.

2. **Connector Plugs:**

- Connector plugs are specific to the cable type (e.g., RJ-45 for Ethernet). They come in various configurations, such as straight-through or crossover.

3. **Cable Cutter/Stripper:**

- These tools are used to trim and strip the cable's outer insulation, exposing the individual wires for termination.

4. **Wire Stripper:**

- A wire stripper is used to remove the insulation from

the individual wires within the cable.

5. **Connector Boots and Strain Relief:**

   - These accessories provide additional protection to the cable and connectors, reducing strain and wear.

Crimping and Termination Techniques for Ethernet Cables (RJ-45):

1. **Prepare the Cable:**

   - Begin by cutting the cable to the desired length, ensuring that it is straight and untangled.

   - Use a cable cutter/stripper to trim the outer insulation, exposing approximately 1.5 inches (3-4 cm) of the cable's inner wires.

2. **Sort and Align Wires:**

   - Sort and arrange the individual wires in the correct order for the specific Ethernet standard (T568A or T568B).

   - Common color codes for Ethernet are: white-orange, orange, white-green, blue, white-blue, green, white-brown, and brown.

3. **Insert Wires into Connector:**

- Carefully insert the wires into the connector plug, ensuring they align with the correct pins inside the plug.

- Ensure that the wires reach the end of the connector.

4. **Crimping:**

- Place the connector and cable into the crimping tool, positioning it correctly.

- Squeeze the crimping tool handles firmly to compress the connector, securing it to the cable.

5. **Check the Termination:**

- After crimping, visually inspect the termination to ensure that all wires are fully seated in the connector, and there is no exposed copper.

- Use a cable tester to verify that the termination is functional and follows the correct pinout.

Best Practices for Crimping and Termination:

- Use high-quality connectors and cables to ensure reliable connections.

- Maintain the correct wire order and alignment when inserting wires into the connector.

- Avoid over-crimping, which can damage the connector or wires.

- Use strain relief boots to prevent cable damage and maintain bend radius specifications.

- Follow the specific wiring standards (T568A or T568B) for Ethernet cables.

- Practice good cable management and labeling to identify cables and terminations accurately.

Safety Precautions:

- Wear appropriate safety gear, such as safety glasses, when working with cables and connectors.

- Exercise caution to prevent injury when using crimping tools and sharp cable-cutting tools.

In conclusion, crimping and termination techniques are fundamental skills in IT infrastructure management, especially in networking and cabling systems. Properly terminated cables ensure reliable connections and efficient data transmission. By following the correct procedures, using the right tools, and adhering to wiring standards, IT professionals can create high-quality terminations that contribute to the overall performance and reliability of their network infrastructure.

D. Best Practices for Hardware Installation in IT Infrastructure

Hardware installation is a critical component of IT infrastructure management, encompassing the deployment of servers, networking equipment, storage devices, and other hardware components. Proper installation ensures the reliability, performance, and longevity of IT systems. In this in-depth exploration, we will delve into best practices for hardware installation in IT infrastructure, covering planning, preparation, safety, and post-installation considerations.

1. Planning and Preparation:

1.1. Site Assessment:

- Conduct a thorough site assessment to evaluate the physical environment, power availability, cooling requirements, and space constraints.

1.2. Hardware Selection:

- Choose hardware components based on the specific needs and workload requirements of the organization.

1.3. Rack and Cabinet Selection:

- Select appropriate server racks or cabinets that can accommodate the hardware and provide adequate ventilation and cable management options.

1.4. Cable Management Planning:

- Plan cable routing and management to maintain neat and organized cabling, reducing the risk of cable-related issues.

1.5. Power Planning:

- Calculate power requirements and ensure that sufficient power outlets and backup power sources are available.

2. Safety Precautions:

2.1. Electrostatic Discharge (ESD) Protection:

- Use ESD protection equipment, such as wrist straps and anti-static mats, to prevent damage to sensitive hardware components.

2.2. Proper Lifting Techniques:

- Train personnel in proper lifting techniques to prevent injuries when handling heavy equipment.

2.3. Electrical Safety:

- Ensure that power sources are properly grounded and adhere to electrical safety guidelines when connecting hardware to power.

2.4. Rack Stability:

- Secure racks and cabinets to prevent tipping or instability, especially when heavy equipment is installed.

3. Installation Procedures:

3.1. Rack Mounting:

- Follow manufacturer instructions for mounting hardware components securely in the rack or cabinet.

3.2. Cable Routing:

- Carefully route and organize cables to prevent tangling and ensure proper airflow.

3.3. Hardware Configuration:

- Configure hardware components according to best practices and industry standards for optimal performance and security.

3.4. Labeling and Documentation:

- Label hardware components and document their locations and configurations for easy identification and troubleshooting.

3.5. Server and Equipment Installation:

- Install servers, switches, routers, and other equipment with attention to proper alignment and ventilation requirements.

4. Testing and Validation:

4.1. Hardware Testing:

- Conduct thorough testing of hardware components to ensure they function as expected before deploying them into production.

4.2. Network Connectivity Testing:

- Verify network connectivity and performance to identify and resolve any issues promptly.

4.3. Documentation Update:

- Update documentation to reflect the newly installed hardware, including IP addresses, configurations, and hardware specifications.

5. Post-Installation Considerations:

5.1. Monitoring and Management:

- Implement monitoring and management tools to continuously

monitor hardware health and performance.

5.2. Maintenance Scheduling:

- Establish a regular maintenance schedule for hardware components to ensure they remain in optimal condition.

5.3. Capacity Planning:

- Continuously assess capacity requirements and plan for future hardware upgrades or expansions.

5.4. Documentation Maintenance:

- Keep hardware documentation up to date, including any changes or modifications made after installation.

5.5. Decommissioning and Disposal:

- Properly decommission and dispose of hardware that has reached the end of its life cycle, following environmental regulations and data security protocols.

In conclusion, following best practices for hardware installation in IT infrastructure is essential for ensuring the stability, performance, and longevity of critical systems. Careful planning, adherence to safety precautions, proper installation procedures, thorough testing, and post-installation considerations are all vital aspects of successful hardware deployment. By implementing these practices, organizations can minimize downtime, reduce operational risks, and maintain a reliable IT infrastructure.

CHAPTER 8

Data Center Setup and Configuration

Data centers serve as the nerve centers of modern organizations, housing critical IT infrastructure and data storage systems. The setup and configuration of a data center are pivotal in ensuring the seamless operation, security, and scalability of an organization's IT environment. In this introductory overview, we will explore the significance of data center setup and configuration, highlighting the key components, considerations, and best practices that contribute to the establishment of a robust and efficient data center.

A well-planned and meticulously configured data center is fundamental to meeting the evolving demands of today's digital landscape. It involves designing and organizing a physical space or virtual environment that encompasses servers, networking equipment, storage solutions, power and cooling systems, and security measures. Effective data center setup and configuration are essential not only for safeguarding critical data but also for achieving high availability, performance optimization, and the ability to adapt to changing technological needs.

In the following sections, we will delve into the intricacies of data center setup and configuration, exploring topics such as initial planning, layout considerations, hardware installation, power and cooling infrastructure, network setup, security measures, documentation, and asset management. By adhering to best practices and staying attuned to industry standards, organizations can ensure that their data center environments are well-prepared to support the ever-growing demands of the digital era.

A. Initial Data Center Planning: The Foundation of a Robust Infrastructure

Initial data center planning is a pivotal phase in the establishment of a reliable and efficient IT infrastructure. This stage involves thorough assessment, strategic decision-making, and precise planning to ensure that the data center can meet the organization's current and future needs. In this in-depth exploration, we will delve into the various aspects and considerations involved in the initial planning of a data center.

1. Needs Assessment:

- **Workload Analysis:** Begin by analyzing the organization's current and projected IT workloads. This analysis should consider factors such as data storage requirements, computational needs, and network traffic patterns.

- **Scalability:** Determine the organization's scalability

requirements. How will the data center accommodate growth in IT demands over time?

2. Location Selection:

- **Site Evaluation:** Carefully select the physical location for the data center. Consider factors such as proximity to staff, accessibility, environmental conditions, and disaster risk assessment.

- **Security:** Evaluate the site's security features and determine if it meets industry standards for physical security.

3. Infrastructure Planning:

- **Power Infrastructure:** Ensure access to reliable and redundant power sources. Implement uninterruptible power supplies (UPS) and backup generators to maintain operations during power outages.

- **Cooling Infrastructure:** Design an efficient cooling system to regulate the temperature within the data center and prevent equipment overheating.

- **Physical Space:** Plan the layout of the data center, including the placement of racks, cabinets, and equipment to maximize space utilization and airflow.

4. Hardware Selection:

- **Server Hardware:** Choose server hardware that aligns with the organization's workload requirements, considering factors like processing power, memory, and storage capacity.

- **Networking Equipment:** Select networking equipment, such as switches and routers, that can handle the expected network traffic and support future expansion.

- **Storage Solutions:** Determine the appropriate storage solutions, including disk arrays and storage area networks (SANs), to meet data storage needs and data access speed requirements.

5. Network Design:

- **Network Architecture:** Define the network architecture, including LAN, WAN, and connectivity to the internet. Ensure redundancy and fault tolerance in network design.

- **IP Addressing:** Plan IP address allocations and subnetting to efficiently manage network resources.

6. Security Measures:

- **Access Control:** Implement strict access control policies to restrict physical and logical access to authorized personnel only.

- **Firewalls and Intrusion Detection:** Deploy firewalls and intrusion detection systems to protect the data center from external threats.

- **Data Encryption:** Enforce data encryption protocols to safeguard sensitive information in transit and at rest.

7. Disaster Recovery and Redundancy:

- **Disaster Recovery Plan:** Develop a comprehensive disaster recovery plan that includes data backups, offsite storage, and recovery procedures to ensure business continuity in case of unexpected events.

- **Redundancy:** Introduce redundancy in critical systems to minimize downtime in the event of hardware or network failures.

8. Documentation and Asset Management:

- **Documentation:** Establish a robust documentation system that includes equipment inventory, network diagrams, IP address records, and configuration documentation.

- **Asset Management:** Implement asset tracking and management systems to monitor hardware components and ensure their maintenance and replacement when necessary.

9. Compliance and Regulations:

- **Compliance:** Ensure that the data center complies with relevant industry regulations, such as data privacy laws and industry-specific standards.

- **Environmental Considerations:** Adhere to environmental regulations and best practices for sustainable data center operation.

10. Budget and Cost Estimation:

- **Cost Estimation:** Prepare a detailed budget that includes equipment costs, construction or renovation expenses, ongoing operational costs, and contingency funds.

- **Cost Optimization:** Explore cost optimization strategies such as virtualization, energy-efficient equipment, and cloud services.

Initial data center planning is a complex process that requires close collaboration between IT professionals, facilities managers, and other stakeholders. It serves as the foundation upon which a robust and resilient data center infrastructure is built. By meticulously addressing each of these considerations, organizations can ensure that their data center is well-equipped to support their IT requirements, maintain high availability, and adapt to evolving technology trends.

B. Layout and Design Considerations for Data Centers

Layout and design considerations play a crucial role in the efficiency, functionality, and scalability of data centers. A well-thought-out layout and design can optimize space utilization, airflow management, and equipment accessibility while ensuring ease of maintenance and future expansion. In this in-depth exploration, we will delve into the key factors and best practices to consider when designing the layout of a data center.

1. Space Planning:

- **Rack Layout:** Decide on the placement and arrangement of server racks or cabinets within the data center. Consider factors such as rack density, airflow, and accessibility.

- **Hot Aisles and Cold Aisles:** Organize racks into hot and cold aisles to facilitate efficient cooling. Cold aisles receive cold air from cooling systems, while hot aisles expel hot air generated by the equipment.

- **Clear Aisles:** Ensure that there are clear, unobstructed aisles for maintenance personnel to access and service equipment.

2. Cooling and Airflow:

- **Cooling Infrastructure:** Position air conditioning units, HVAC systems, or other cooling solutions strategically to distribute cool air effectively to equipment.

- **Airflow Management:** Implement measures such as raised floors, containment systems, and blanking panels to manage airflow and minimize hotspots.

- **Temperature Monitoring:** Install temperature sensors and monitoring systems to track temperature variations within the data center and make real-time adjustments as needed.

3. Power Distribution:

- **Power Distribution Units (PDUs):** Deploy PDUs at appropriate locations to distribute power to racks and cabinets efficiently. Consider redundancy and load balancing.

- **Cable Management:** Use cable management systems to keep power cables organized and prevent interference with airflow.

4. Rack and Cabinet Selection:

- **Rack Dimensions:** Choose rack dimensions that align with the size and weight of the equipment to be housed. Standard rack widths are 19 inches, while heights can vary.

- **Cabinet Features:** Consider cabinets with features like locking doors, perforated doors for ventilation, and cable management options.

5. Redundancy and High Availability:

- **Redundant Systems:** Design with redundancy in mind to ensure continuous operation in case of component failures. This includes redundant power supplies, network connections, and cooling.

- **Fault Tolerance:** Implement fault-tolerant configurations to minimize the risk of downtime due to hardware failures.

6. Security Measures:

- **Physical Security:** Incorporate physical security measures such as access control systems, surveillance cameras, and biometric authentication to restrict unauthorized access.

- **Secure Cabinets:** Ensure that server cabinets and racks are lockable to prevent tampering or theft of equipment.

7. Expansion and Scalability:

- **Scalable Design:** Plan for future expansion by leaving adequate space for additional racks, cabinets, and cooling units.

- **Modular Design:** Consider modular designs that allow for easy integration of new equipment and scalability without major disruptions.

8. Fire Suppression and Safety:

- **Fire Suppression Systems:** Install fire suppression systems that are suitable for data center environments, such as clean agent systems that minimize damage to equipment.

- **Safety Procedures:** Establish safety protocols and conduct regular safety drills to ensure personnel know how to respond in case of emergencies.

9. Documentation and Labeling:

- **Documentation:** Maintain detailed documentation of the data center layout, equipment inventory, cabling, and network diagrams.

- **Labeling:** Label racks, cables, and equipment with clear and standardized labeling to simplify troubleshooting and maintenance.

10. Compliance and Regulations:

- **Compliance:** Ensure that the data center design complies with industry standards, regulations, and environmental guidelines.

11. Environmental Considerations:

- **Energy Efficiency:** Implement energy-efficient technologies and practices to reduce power consumption and minimize the environmental impact.

- **Sustainable Design:** Explore sustainable design options, such as free cooling, to reduce the carbon footprint of the data center.

12. Accessibility and Ergonomics:

- **Workspaces:** Design workspaces for IT personnel with ergonomic considerations to promote comfort and productivity.

- **Accessibility:** Ensure that equipment and cabling are accessible for maintenance and troubleshooting without physical strain.

Data center layout and design require careful planning, collaboration among various stakeholders, and adherence to industry best practices. An efficient and well-designed data center not only enhances performance and reliability but also provides the flexibility needed to adapt to changing technology trends and business requirements.

C. Installation of Racks and Hardware in Data Centers

The installation of racks and hardware is a fundamental aspect of data center setup and plays a critical role in determining the efficiency, organization, and accessibility of IT infrastructure. Racks and cabinets provide the framework for housing servers, networking equipment, storage devices, and other hardware components. In this in-depth exploration, we will delve into the best practices and considerations for the installation of racks and hardware in data centers.

1. Rack and Cabinet Selection:

- **Choose the Right Rack:** Select racks or cabinets that meet the specific requirements of your data center, including dimensions, weight capacity, and features such as cable management options, perforated doors for ventilation, and locking mechanisms.

- **Standard Rack Sizes:** Consider standard rack sizes, typically 19 inches wide, for compatibility with industry-standard hardware.

2. Space Planning:

- **Positioning Racks:** Plan the placement and arrangement of racks within the data center. Ensure that racks are spaced to allow for proper airflow, accessibility, and maintenance.

- **Rack Density:** Determine the rack density based on the power and cooling capacity of the data center. Avoid overcrowding racks, which can lead to overheating.

3. Rack Installation:

- **Secure Mounting:** Use appropriate mounting hardware, such as cage nuts and screws, to securely attach racks to the data center floor or raised floor tiles. Ensure that racks are level and stable.

- **Redundancy:** Implement rack-level redundancy if needed, such as dual power feeds and network connections to ensure high availability.

4. Cable Management:

- **Cable Routing:** Plan and implement cable routing within the racks to maintain organization, prevent cable tangling, and optimize airflow.

- **Cable Management Accessories:** Use cable management accessories, such as horizontal and vertical cable managers, to keep cables organized and secure.

5. Server Hardware Installation:

- **Proper Handling:** Follow manufacturer guidelines for handling and installing server hardware to avoid damage.

- **Equipment Rails:** Use equipment rails and shelves designed for specific server models to ensure proper fit and secure installation.

- **Rack Units:** Ensure that servers are installed at the appropriate rack units (U) to maximize space utilization.

6. Networking Equipment Installation:

- **Switches and Routers:** Mount switches and routers in rack units designed to accommodate network equipment. Pay attention to cable management for network connections.

7. Cable Installation:

- **Structured Cabling:** Follow structured cabling standards to install data, power, and fiber optic cables neatly and efficiently.

- **Labeling:** Label cables and connectors clearly and consistently to simplify troubleshooting and maintenance.

8. Cooling Considerations:

- **Position for Airflow:** Install equipment within racks to optimize airflow, with front-facing equipment drawing in cool air and rear exhausts directing hot air away from adjacent equipment.

- **Temperature Sensors:** Use temperature sensors to monitor the temperature within racks and adjust cooling systems as needed.

9. Security Measures:

- **Locking Mechanisms:** Ensure that racks and cabinets have locking mechanisms to prevent unauthorized access to equipment.

10. Accessibility and Safety:

- **Clear Aisles:** Maintain clear aisles and pathways to allow easy access to equipment for maintenance and emergency situations.

- **Safety Precautions:** Enforce safety protocols for personnel working in and around racks, including proper lifting techniques and ESD protection.

11. Documentation and Asset Management:

- **Documentation:** Keep detailed records of equipment installation, including serial numbers, configurations, and locations within the racks.

- **Asset Tracking:** Implement an asset tracking system to monitor the status and maintenance schedules of hardware components.

12. Compliance and Regulations:

- **Regulatory Compliance:** Ensure that equipment installation complies with industry-specific regulations and standards.

Proper installation of racks and hardware is essential for maintaining the reliability and functionality of a data center. By adhering to best practices, organizations can ensure that their data center infrastructure is organized, accessible, and designed to support current and future IT needs while minimizing downtime and operational risks.

D. Power and Cooling Infrastructure in Data Centers: Ensuring Efficiency and Reliability

Power and cooling infrastructure are the lifelines of data centers, essential for maintaining the reliability and performance of IT equipment. Data centers house racks of servers, networking devices, storage systems, and other hardware that generate significant heat and require stable power sources. In this in-depth exploration, we will delve into the critical aspects and best practices of power and cooling infrastructure in data centers.

1. Power Infrastructure:

1.1. Power Sources:

- **Primary Power:** Data centers typically rely on primary power sources from the grid. Ensure that this power source is stable, with minimal disruptions.

- **Redundant Power:** Implement redundant power sources, such as backup generators and uninterruptible power supplies

(UPS), to maintain operations during power outages.

1.2. Power Distribution:

- **Power Distribution Units (PDUs):** Use PDUs to distribute power to racks and cabinets efficiently. Consider intelligent PDUs that provide real-time power consumption data.

- **Redundancy:** Implement redundancy in power distribution to avoid single points of failure. Dual power feeds to each rack or cabinet are common for redundancy.

1.3. Energy Efficiency:

- **Energy-Efficient Equipment:** Choose energy-efficient hardware, including servers and cooling systems, to reduce overall power consumption.

- **Hot Aisle/Cold Aisle:** Organize racks into hot and cold aisles to optimize cooling and reduce the need for excess cooling.

1.4. Power Monitoring:

- **Monitoring Systems:** Install power monitoring systems to track energy consumption, detect abnormalities, and optimize power usage.

2. Cooling Infrastructure:

2.1. Cooling Systems:

- **Precision Air Conditioning:** Implement precision cooling systems that maintain a controlled temperature and humidity level within the data center.

- **Hot/Cold Aisle Containment:** Use hot/cold aisle containment to segregate hot and cold airflows, preventing recirculation of hot air to cooling inlets.

2.2. Redundancy and Failover:

- **Redundant Cooling:** Ensure redundancy in cooling systems to prevent overheating in case of system failures.

- **Temperature Sensors:** Install temperature sensors throughout the data center to monitor and control cooling based on real-time conditions.

2.3. Energy Efficiency:

- **Free Cooling:** Explore free cooling methods, such as air-side or water-side economizers, to reduce energy consumption.

- **Hot Water Cooling:** Consider advanced cooling techniques like hot water cooling, which can be more energy-efficient.

2.4. Cooling Best Practices:

- **Cable Management:** Proper cable management can improve airflow and cooling efficiency.

- **Hot Spot Detection:** Use thermal imaging or other tools to identify hot spots and optimize cooling.

3. Maintenance and Monitoring:

3.1. Regular Maintenance:

- **Scheduled Inspections:** Schedule regular inspections and maintenance of power and cooling systems to identify and address issues proactively.

3.2. Monitoring Systems:

- **Real-time Monitoring:** Implement real-time monitoring systems to track power usage, temperature, and humidity and receive alerts for anomalies.

4. Environmental Considerations:

4.1. Environmental Impact:

- **Sustainability:** Consider sustainability efforts, such as using renewable energy sources, to reduce the environmental impact of data center operations.

4.2. Heat Reuse:

- **Heat Recovery:** Explore heat recovery systems that can repurpose excess heat generated by data center equipment for other purposes, such as heating nearby buildings.

5. Documentation and Compliance:

5.1. Documentation:

- **Maintain Records:** Keep detailed records of power and cooling configurations, maintenance schedules, and system performance.

5.2. Compliance:

- **Regulatory Compliance:** Ensure that power and cooling systems meet industry standards and regulatory requirements, particularly in sectors with strict compliance rules, such as healthcare or finance.

Power and cooling infrastructure are critical components of data center operations. Ensuring the efficiency, redundancy, and reliability of these systems is essential for maintaining the integrity and availability of IT equipment. By implementing best practices, organizations can optimize energy usage, reduce operational risks, and extend the lifespan of their data center infrastructure.

E. Network Infrastructure Setup: Building a Solid Foundation for Data Center Connectivity

The network infrastructure setup in a data center is the backbone that enables communication, data transfer, and connectivity for all IT equipment within the facility. A well-designed and properly configured network infrastructure is critical for ensuring data center reliability, performance, and security. In this in-depth exploration, we will delve into the essential components, considerations, and best practices for setting up network infrastructure in a data center.

1. Network Architecture:

1.1. LAN (Local Area Network):

- **Segmentation:** Divide the LAN into logical segments to isolate traffic and improve network performance. This includes VLANs (Virtual LANs) for separating different groups of devices.

- **Switching:** Deploy high-performance Ethernet switches to facilitate fast and reliable data transmission within the LAN.

1.2. WAN (Wide Area Network):

- **Connectivity:** Establish WAN connections to link the data center with remote sites, branches, or the internet. Consider redundant connections for high availability.

- **Routing:** Configure routers to manage traffic between different networks and optimize routing protocols for efficient data transfer.

1.3. VPN (Virtual Private Network):

- **Security:** Implement VPN solutions for secure remote access to the data center network, ensuring data confidentiality and integrity.

2. Network Hardware:

2.1. Routers:

- **Core Routers:** Install core routers to manage traffic between LAN segments and WAN connections, providing scalability and redundancy.

2.2. Switches:

- **Layer 2 and Layer 3 Switches:** Use Layer 2 switches for local network segments and Layer 3 switches for routing and VLAN management.

- **Redundancy:** Deploy redundant switches with failover capabilities to minimize network downtime.

2.3. Firewalls:

- **Firewall Appliances:** Install firewall appliances to secure incoming and outgoing network traffic, applying access control policies and intrusion detection.

2.4. Load Balancers:

- **Application Load Balancers (ALBs):** Employ ALBs to distribute network traffic evenly across multiple servers, optimizing resource utilization and ensuring high availability.

3. IP Addressing and Subnetting:

- **IP Address Management:** Implement an IP address management (IPAM) system to efficiently allocate and manage IP addresses within the data center.

- **Subnet Design:** Design subnets logically to streamline network administration and minimize broadcast domains.

4. Redundancy and High Availability:

- **Redundancy:** Set up redundant network paths, switches, and routers to eliminate single points of failure and ensure uninterrupted network connectivity.

- **Failover Mechanisms:** Implement failover mechanisms and protocols, such as HSRP (Hot Standby Router Protocol) or VRRP (Virtual Router Redundancy Protocol), for router redundancy.

5. Network Security:

5.1. Access Control:

- **Access Control Lists (ACLs):** Define ACLs to restrict access to network resources based on source IP addresses, ports, or protocols.

- **Authentication:** Enforce strong authentication methods for network access, such as 802.1X, and use multifactor authentication where appropriate.

5.2. Intrusion Detection and Prevention:

- **Intrusion Detection Systems (IDS):** Deploy IDS solutions to monitor network traffic for suspicious activities and generate alerts.

- **Intrusion Prevention Systems (IPS):** Utilize IPS to actively block or mitigate security threats.

6. Network Monitoring and Management:

- **Monitoring Tools:** Implement network monitoring tools and solutions to continuously assess network health, identify performance bottlenecks, and troubleshoot issues.

- **Configuration Management:** Use configuration management tools to automate network configuration changes and maintain consistency.

7. Scalability and Growth:

- **Scalable Design:** Plan for scalability by designing the network infrastructure to accommodate additional devices, increased traffic, and future expansion.

8. Documentation and Change Management:

- **Documentation:** Maintain detailed documentation of network configurations, diagrams, IP address assignments, and hardware inventory.

- **Change Control:** Enforce change control procedures to track and approve network configuration changes to prevent disruptions.

9. Compliance and Regulations:

- **Compliance:** Ensure that network setup and configurations adhere to industry-specific regulations and compliance standards, such as HIPAA, GDPR, or PCI DSS.

The network infrastructure setup in a data center is a complex and critical task that requires careful planning, expertise, and adherence to best practices. A well-structured and robust network design is essential for supporting the diverse requirements of modern IT environments, facilitating efficient data transfer, and ensuring the security and reliability of data center operations.

F. Security Measures for Data Centers: Safeguarding the Digital Fortress

Data centers are high-value targets for cyberattacks and physical threats due to the critical information they house. Implementing comprehensive security measures is paramount to protect against unauthorized access, data breaches, and disruptions. In this in-depth exploration, we will delve into the essential security measures and best practices for safeguarding data centers.

1. Physical Security:

1.1. Access Control:

- **Biometric Authentication:** Implement biometric systems (e.g., fingerprint, retina scans) for authorized personnel access.

- **Access Cards:** Use access cards with multifactor authentication for entry points and restricted areas.

- **Surveillance Cameras:** Deploy surveillance cameras at critical entry and exit points for monitoring and recording.

1.2. Perimeter Security:

- **Fencing and Barriers:** Install robust perimeter fencing and barriers to deter unauthorized access to the data center premises.

- **Gates and Turnstiles:** Control entry and exit points with secure gates and turnstiles.

- **Vehicle Access:** Manage and monitor vehicle access through controlled checkpoints.

1.3. Intrusion Detection:

- **Intrusion Alarm Systems:** Implement intrusion detection systems to detect unauthorized access attempts and trigger alerts.

- **Motion Sensors:** Use motion sensors in critical areas to detect unauthorized movement.

1.4. Mantraps: Set up mantrap systems that require dual authentication for entry, ensuring that only one person can enter or exit at a time.

1.5. Security Personnel: Employ trained security personnel to monitor access points and respond to incidents.

1.6. Bollards and Anti-ram Barriers: Install bollards and anti-ram barriers to protect against vehicle-based attacks.

2. Network Security:

2.1. Firewalls:

- **Perimeter Firewalls:** Implement perimeter firewalls to

control incoming and outgoing network traffic.

- **Application Firewalls:** Use application layer firewalls to inspect and filter traffic at the application level.

2.2. Intrusion Detection and Prevention:

- **Intrusion Detection Systems (IDS):** Deploy IDS to monitor network traffic for suspicious activities.

- **Intrusion Prevention Systems (IPS):** Utilize IPS to actively block or mitigate security threats.

2.3. Network Segmentation: Segment the network to limit lateral movement in case of a breach. This includes VLANs and micro-segmentation.

2.4. VPN and Encryption: Require the use of virtual private networks (VPNs) for remote access, and ensure that data in transit is encrypted.

2.5. DDoS Mitigation: Implement distributed denial-of-service (DDoS) mitigation strategies to protect against large-scale attacks.

3. Cybersecurity:

3.1. Patch Management: Keep all software and firmware up to date with security patches to address known vulnerabilities.

3.2. Security Awareness Training: Train personnel to recognize and respond to security threats, including social engineering attacks.

3.3. Security Information and Event Management (SIEM): Deploy SIEM solutions to collect, analyze, and correlate security event data.

4. Environmental Controls:

4.1. Fire Suppression Systems: Install fire suppression systems that are safe for data center environments, such as clean agent systems.

4.2. Climate Control: Maintain stable temperature and humidity levels to prevent equipment overheating and corrosion.

4.3. Environmental Monitoring: Use environmental sensors to detect and alert on conditions like water leaks or smoke.

5. Redundancy and Backup:

5.1. Redundant Power and Connectivity: Ensure redundant power sources and network connections to maintain operations during outages.

5.2. Data Backup and Recovery: Regularly back up data, and implement a robust data recovery plan.

6. Compliance and Auditing:

- **Regular Audits:** Conduct security audits and assessments to ensure compliance with industry-specific regulations and standards.

7. Incident Response Plan:

- **Develop an incident response plan:** Clearly define roles and responsibilities for responding to security incidents and regularly test the plan through drills and simulations.

Comprehensive security measures for data centers encompass both physical and digital aspects. The combination of access controls, network security, cybersecurity practices, environmental controls, redundancy, and incident response plans creates a robust defense against a wide range of threats, from physical breaches to cyberattacks. Data center security is an ongoing process, requiring continuous monitoring, updates, and adaptability to address emerging threats and vulnerabilities.

G. Documentation and Asset Management for Data Centers: The Foundation of Operational Excellence

Effective documentation and asset management are the cornerstones of efficient data center operations. In a data center environment, where complex systems and equipment interconnect, keeping accurate records and managing assets diligently is essential for maintaining reliability, troubleshooting issues, and ensuring compliance. In this in-depth exploration, we will delve into the critical aspects and best practices of documentation and asset management in data centers.

1. Documentation Practices:

1.1. Inventory Documentation:

- **Asset Inventory:** Maintain an up-to-date inventory of all hardware and software assets within the data center, including servers, networking equipment, storage devices, and applications.

- **Configuration Documentation:** Create detailed configuration documentation for each asset, specifying hardware specifications, network configurations, and software versions.

1.2. Network Diagrams:

- **Network Topology:** Develop network topology diagrams that illustrate the layout of networking equipment, connections, and data flows within the data center.

- **IP Addressing Schemes:** Document IP addressing schemes, VLAN assignments, and subnet configurations to ensure accurate network management.

1.3. Cable Management:

- **Cable Layout Diagrams:** Create cable layout diagrams that depict the routing and organization of data, power, and fiber optic cables within racks and cabinets.

- **Labeling:** Label all cables with clear and standardized labels to simplify troubleshooting and maintenance.

1.4. Change Management:

- **Change Records:** Maintain a record of all changes made to the data center environment, including equipment installations, configurations, and updates.

- **Change Approval:** Implement a change approval process to ensure that changes are reviewed, authorized, and documented.

1.5. Standard Operating Procedures (SOPs):

- **SOP Documentation:** Develop and document standard operating procedures for routine tasks, maintenance procedures, and incident response protocols.

1.6. Compliance Documentation:

- **Regulatory Compliance:** Document compliance with industry-specific regulations and standards, such as HIPAA, GDPR, or PCI DSS.

1.7. Incident Response Plan:

- **Response Documentation:** Create documentation outlining the steps to be taken in the event of a security incident or data breach.

- **Post-Incident Review:** After an incident, conduct a post-incident review and document lessons learned and actions taken for improvement.

2. Asset Management Practices:

2.1. Asset Identification:

- **Asset Tags:** Attach unique asset tags or barcodes to all hardware equipment for easy identification and tracking.

- **Asset Naming Conventions:** Establish naming conventions for assets to ensure consistency and clarity.

2.2. Asset Tracking:

- **Asset Database:** Maintain an asset management database or system that records asset details, such as purchase date, warranty information, location, and owner.

- **Lifecycle Management:** Implement asset lifecycle management processes, including procurement, deployment, maintenance, and retirement or disposal.

2.3. Asset Monitoring:

- **Real-time Monitoring:** Utilize asset monitoring tools to track the status, performance, and health of critical equipment.

2.4. Asset Audits:

- **Regular Audits:** Conduct regular asset audits to reconcile physical assets with the asset database and identify discrepancies.

2.5. Maintenance Records:

- **Maintenance History:** Keep records of maintenance activities, including dates, descriptions, and outcomes, to track equipment health and performance.

2.6. Decommissioning and Disposal:

- **Proper Disposal:** Follow proper disposal procedures for retired equipment, ensuring data security and environmental compliance.

2.7. Access Control:

- **Access Permissions:** Implement access controls to restrict physical and logical access to data center assets.

Effective documentation and asset management practices are instrumental in ensuring data center efficiency, reliability, and compliance. By maintaining accurate records, tracking assets throughout their lifecycle, and adhering to standardized procedures, data center operators can streamline operations, reduce downtime, enhance security, and demonstrate compliance with regulatory requirements. Continuous monitoring, regular audits, and the integration of asset management tools further contribute to operational excellence in data center management.

CHAPTER 9

Cloud Infrastructure Management: Navigating the Digital Skyline

Cloud infrastructure management is at the forefront of modern IT operations, revolutionizing the way organizations build, scale, and maintain their digital resources. As businesses increasingly migrate to cloud platforms, the need for effective management of cloud infrastructure becomes paramount. In this introductory exploration, we will embark on a journey through the realms of cloud infrastructure management, uncovering the fundamental principles, challenges, and opportunities it presents in today's technology landscape.

Cloud infrastructure management involves the orchestration and governance of a dynamic and scalable network of virtualized servers, storage, networking, and services hosted across cloud providers' data centers. Whether it's public, private, or hybrid cloud environments, organizations must master the art of efficiently provisioning resources, optimizing costs, ensuring security, and meeting performance demands to thrive in the cloud era.

This journey will take us through the key pillars of cloud infrastructure management, including provisioning and scaling, security and compliance, cost optimization, monitoring and performance management, and the strategic considerations involved in selecting the right cloud models and services to meet business objectives. Whether you are a seasoned cloud architect or just embarking on your cloud journey, our exploration of cloud infrastructure management will provide insights, strategies, and best practices to navigate the digital skyline with confidence and precision.

A. Cloud Service Models (IaaS, PaaS, SaaS): Unveiling the Layers of Cloud Computing

Cloud computing has transformed the way businesses and individuals access and manage digital resources. At the heart of cloud computing lie three fundamental service models: Infrastructure as a Service (IaaS), Platform as a Service (PaaS), and Software as a Service (SaaS). These service models form the building blocks of the cloud ecosystem, each offering distinct capabilities and advantages. In this in-depth exploration, we will dissect each of these cloud service models, shedding light on their features, use cases, and the value they bring to businesses and end-users.

1. Infrastructure as a Service (IaaS):

1.1. Core Concept:

IaaS represents the foundational layer of cloud computing, providing users with virtualized computing resources over the internet. These resources typically include virtual machines, storage, and networking components.

1.2. Key Features:

- **On-Demand Resources:** Users can provision and de-provision virtual resources as needed, paying only for what they use.

- **Scalability:** IaaS platforms offer the flexibility to scale resources up or down based on workload demands.

- **Resource Management:** Users have control over operating systems, applications, and network configurations.

1.3. Use Cases:

- **Development and Testing:** Developers can quickly create and tear down virtual environments for software development and testing.

- **Disaster Recovery:** IaaS can serve as a cost-effective solution for disaster recovery, providing backup resources in the cloud.

2. Platform as a Service (PaaS):

2.1. Core Concept:

PaaS builds on IaaS by offering a comprehensive platform that includes not only infrastructure but also development tools, databases, and runtime environments for building, deploying, and managing applications.

2.2. Key Features:

- **Application Development:** PaaS provides tools and services for application development, such as programming languages, databases, and integrated development environments.

- **Scalability:** Like IaaS, PaaS platforms offer scalability, but they abstract much of the underlying infrastructure management.

- **Managed Services:** PaaS providers handle much of the backend infrastructure management, allowing developers to focus on coding.

2.3. Use Cases:

- **Web Application Development:** Developers can build web applications, APIs, and microservices using PaaS platforms.

- **Data Analysis:** PaaS can be used for data analytics and processing, with access to tools and resources for big data projects.

3. Software as a Service (SaaS):

3.1. Core Concept:

SaaS represents the top layer of cloud computing, delivering fully functional software applications over the internet. Users access these applications through web browsers without the need for installation or maintenance.

3.2. Key Features:

- **Accessibility:** SaaS applications are accessible from any device with an internet connection and a web browser.

- **Automatic Updates:** SaaS providers handle software updates and maintenance, ensuring users always have access to the latest features and security patches.

- **Multi-Tenancy:** Providers serve multiple customers from a shared infrastructure, optimizing resource utilization.

3.3. Use Cases:

- **Email and Productivity Tools:** Common examples of SaaS include email services (e.g., Gmail) and productivity suites (e.g., Microsoft 365).

- **Customer Relationship Management (CRM):** Businesses

use SaaS CRM solutions like Salesforce for managing customer relationships.

Choosing the Right Service Model:

- **Considerations:** The choice between IaaS, PaaS, and SaaS depends on factors like your organization's IT capabilities, development needs, scalability requirements, and cost constraints.

- **Hybrid Cloud:** Many organizations leverage a combination of these service models in a hybrid cloud approach to meet diverse needs.

- **Integration:** Ensure that the chosen service model aligns with your existing infrastructure and can seamlessly integrate with your other IT systems.

Cloud service models IaaS, PaaS, and SaaS provide a spectrum of options for organizations to harness the benefits of cloud computing while addressing specific business requirements. Whether you need the foundational infrastructure, a robust development platform, or fully managed software applications, the cloud service models offer the flexibility and scalability to propel your digital initiatives forward.

B. Cloud Deployment Models (Public, Private,

Hybrid): Navigating the Cloud Landscape

When adopting cloud computing, organizations must make strategic decisions about how to deploy their workloads and data. Cloud deployment models offer different approaches to where and how IT resources are hosted and managed. The three primary cloud deployment models are Public Cloud, Private Cloud, and Hybrid Cloud. In this in-depth exploration, we will dissect each of these models, highlighting their characteristics, use cases, and the considerations that guide organizations in choosing the right approach for their specific needs.

1. Public Cloud:

1.1. Core Concept:

Public Cloud is a cloud computing model where cloud resources, such as virtual machines, storage, and applications, are owned and operated by a third-party cloud service provider and made available to the general public over the internet. These resources are typically delivered on a pay-as-you-go or subscription basis.

1.2. Key Features:

- **Scalability:** Public clouds offer virtually limitless scalability, allowing organizations to quickly provision and de-provision resources as needed.

- **Shared Resources:** Public clouds are multi-tenant environments, meaning multiple customers share the same infrastructure, which optimizes resource utilization and lowers costs.

- **Managed Services:** Public cloud providers handle most of the infrastructure management tasks, including hardware maintenance and security.

1.3. Use Cases:

- **Web Applications:** Hosting web applications, websites, and content delivery.

- **Development and Testing:** Quickly creating development and testing environments.

2. Private Cloud:

2.1. Core Concept:

Private Cloud is a cloud deployment model where cloud resources are used exclusively by a single organization. These resources can be hosted on-premises or by a third-party provider and are often managed and customized to meet the specific needs of the organization.

2.2. Key Features:

- **Isolation:** Private clouds offer dedicated resources, ensuring data and workloads are isolated from other organizations.

- **Control:** Organizations have full control over the infrastructure, allowing for customization, security, and compliance enforcement.

- **Data Privacy:** Private clouds are favored by organizations with stringent data privacy and regulatory requirements.

2.3. Use Cases:

- **Sensitive Data:** Storing and processing sensitive data, such as healthcare or financial records.

- **Regulatory Compliance:** Meeting regulatory requirements, like HIPAA or GDPR.

3. Hybrid Cloud:

3.1. Core Concept:

Hybrid Cloud is a cloud deployment model that combines elements of both public and private clouds. It allows data and applications to be shared between them, providing greater flexibility and more deployment options.

3.2. Key Features:

- **Interoperability:** Hybrid clouds enable data and workloads to move seamlessly between public and private environments.

- **Scalability:** Organizations can scale workloads dynamically between public and private clouds based on demand.

- **Data Replication:** Data can be replicated or synchronized between public and private clouds for redundancy and disaster recovery.

3.3. Use Cases:

- **Bursting:** Handling spikes in demand by using public cloud resources when private cloud capacity is exceeded.

- **Disaster Recovery:** Ensuring data redundancy and disaster recovery through a hybrid approach.

Choosing the Right Deployment Model:

- **Considerations:** The choice between public, private, or hybrid deployment models depends on factors such as data sensitivity, regulatory compliance, scalability needs, and budget constraints.

- **Cost Analysis:** Evaluate the total cost of ownership (TCO) and return on investment (ROI) for each deployment model.

- **Data Governance:** Consider data governance and compliance requirements when selecting a deployment model.

- **Flexibility:** Assess the need for flexibility and the ability to scale resources up or down as business needs change.

Cloud deployment models offer a spectrum of options for organizations to align their cloud strategy with their specific business objectives and constraints. Public clouds provide scale and cost-efficiency, private clouds offer control and security, and hybrid clouds combine the best of both worlds. A strategic approach to cloud deployment can unlock the full potential of cloud computing while addressing the unique needs and challenges of the organization.

C. Managing Multi-Cloud Environments: Orchestrating the Cloud Symphony

In today's dynamic technology landscape, many organizations are adopting a multi-cloud strategy to leverage the strengths of different cloud providers while minimizing vendor lock-in and enhancing flexibility. Managing multi-cloud environments, however, introduces complexities related to resource orchestration, security, cost optimization, and governance. In this in-depth exploration, we will dive into the challenges and best practices of managing multi-cloud environments to ensure seamless operations and maximize the benefits of this strategy.

1. Resource Orchestration:

1.1. Cloud Resource Abstraction:

- **Orchestration Tools:** Utilize cloud orchestration tools like

Terraform, AWS CloudFormation, or Azure Resource Manager to abstract cloud-specific configurations, making it easier to manage resources across different providers.

- **Infrastructure as Code (IaC):** Implement IaC principles to define and provision resources programmatically, ensuring consistency and reproducibility.

1.2. Resource Portability:

- **Containers:** Embrace containerization and container orchestration platforms like Kubernetes to enhance resource portability across clouds.

- **Serverless Computing:** Consider serverless computing options that abstract the underlying infrastructure, reducing cloud provider dependencies.

2. Security and Compliance:

2.1. Identity and Access Management (IAM):

- **Centralized IAM:** Implement a centralized IAM solution that manages user access and permissions consistently across all cloud providers.

- **Single Sign-On (SSO):** Use SSO solutions to simplify user authentication and access control.

2.2. Network Security:

- **Virtual Private Clouds (VPCs):** Isolate network resources using VPCs, VNet, or similar constructs provided by cloud providers.

- **Network Security Groups (NSGs):** Define NSGs to control inbound and outbound traffic to virtual networks.

2.3. Compliance Management:

- **Compliance Tools:** Leverage compliance management tools to monitor and enforce regulatory requirements across multi-cloud environments.

3. Cost Optimization:

3.1. Cost Visibility:

- **Cost Management Tools:** Employ cost management tools and services provided by cloud providers to gain visibility into spending across different clouds.

- **Cost Allocation:** Allocate costs accurately to different departments or projects using tags or labels.

3.2. Reserved Instances (RIs) and Spot Instances:

- **RIs:** Purchase RIs to commit to a certain amount of compute capacity, reducing costs in the long term.

- **Spot Instances:** Use spot instances for non-critical workloads to take advantage of cost savings when resources are available.

4. Governance and Compliance:

4.1. Cloud Management Platforms:

- **Cloud Management Platforms (CMPs):** Consider using CMPs to centralize governance, manage policies, and ensure compliance across multi-cloud environments.

4.2. Policy as Code:

- **Policy as Code (PaC):** Define governance policies as code to automate compliance checks and enforce policies consistently.

5. Monitoring and Performance Management:

5.1. Multi-Cloud Monitoring Tools:

- **Monitoring Tools:** Implement multi-cloud monitoring solutions to gain visibility into performance and health metrics across different cloud providers.

5.2. Service-Level Objectives (SLOs):

- **SLOs and SLIs:** Define service-level objectives and service-level indicators to set performance expectations and monitor compliance.

6. Vendor Management:

6.1. Vendor Relationships:

- **Vendor Partnerships:** Cultivate strong relationships with cloud providers and engage with their support teams for assistance and optimization recommendations.

6.2. Exit Strategy:

- **Exit Plan:** Develop an exit strategy that includes data migration and resource decommissioning plans to mitigate vendor lock-in risks.

Managing multi-cloud environments is a complex endeavor, but when executed strategically, it can yield significant benefits in terms of flexibility, performance, and cost optimization. A well-orchestrated multi-cloud strategy, backed by robust resource orchestration, security measures, cost optimization, governance, and effective monitoring, empowers organizations to harness the full potential of multi-cloud environments while mitigating challenges and risks.

D. Cost Optimization in the Cloud: Maximizing Efficiency and Value

Cost optimization in the cloud is a critical aspect of cloud management, as it ensures that organizations get the most value out of their cloud investments while controlling expenses. Cloud services provide scalability, flexibility, and agility, but without proper cost management, bills can quickly spiral out of control. In this in-depth exploration, we will delve into the strategies, best practices, and tools that organizations can leverage to optimize their cloud spending.

1. Rightsize Resources:

1.1. Resource Utilization:

- **Monitoring and Analysis:** Utilize cloud monitoring tools to track resource utilization and identify underutilized or overprovisioned resources.

- **Auto-scaling:** Implement auto-scaling policies to dynamically adjust resources based on workload demand, reducing overprovisioning.

1.2. Reserved Instances (RIs):

- **RI Planning:** Assess workloads that have stable and predictable usage patterns, and purchase RIs to benefit from cost savings.

- **RI Management:** Continuously review and adjust RI purchases to match evolving workload requirements.

2. Cloud Cost Visibility:

2.1. Cost Monitoring:

- **Cloud Cost Management Tools:** Use cloud cost management and optimization tools provided by cloud providers or third-party solutions to gain insight into spending.

- **Tagging:** Implement tagging strategies to categorize resources and allocate costs accurately to departments or projects.

2.2. Budgets and Alerts:

- **Budget Setting:** Establish cloud cost budgets and configure alerts to receive notifications when costs approach predefined thresholds.

3. Resource Allocation:

3.1. Spot Instances and Preemptible VMs:

- **Spot Instances (AWS) and Preemptible VMs (GCP):** Leverage these low-cost, short-lived instances for non-critical workloads when downtime is acceptable.

3.2. Resource Sharing:

- **Resource Sharing:** Share resources, such as databases and storage, across multiple workloads or teams to optimize resource utilization.

4. Data Storage Optimization:

4.1. Data Lifecycle Management:

- **Data Tiering:** Implement data tiering strategies to move less frequently accessed data to lower-cost storage tiers.

- **Data Deletion:** Regularly delete redundant or obsolete data to reduce storage costs.

4.2. Data Compression and Deduplication:

- **Data Optimization Tools:** Use compression and deduplication tools to reduce the amount of storage space required.

5. Cloud Cost Governance:

5.1. Cost Allocation:

- **Cost Allocation:** Establish clear cost allocation practices to attribute cloud costs to specific projects, departments, or teams.

5.2. Policy Enforcement:

- **Policy as Code (PaC):** Implement policy as code to automate governance rules, such as resource tagging or budget enforcement.

6. Cost Analysis and Reporting:

6.1. Regular Review:

- **Cost Review:** Regularly review cloud cost reports, analyze trends, and identify areas for optimization.

6.2. Cost Optimization Teams:

- **Cloud Cost Optimization Teams:** Establish cross-functional teams responsible for monitoring, optimizing, and reporting on cloud costs.

7. Cloud Vendor Negotiations:

7.1. Negotiation Strategies:

- **Vendor Relationships:** Leverage relationships with cloud providers to negotiate better pricing and contract terms.

7.2. Discounts and Commitments:

- **Volume Discounts:** Consider volume discounts or commitments for long-term usage to reduce costs.

8. Continuous Improvement:

8.1. Cost Optimization Culture:

- **Culture of Optimization:** Foster a culture of continuous cost optimization, where teams are encouraged to find ways to improve efficiency.

8.2. Training and Awareness:

- **Training and Awareness:** Invest in training and awareness programs to educate teams on cost optimization best practices.

Cost optimization in the cloud is an ongoing process that requires vigilance, monitoring, and adaptation as workloads and business needs evolve. By implementing these strategies and best practices, organizations can effectively manage and optimize their cloud spending, ensuring that the cloud remains a cost-effective and valuable resource for their digital initiatives.

E. Cloud Security and Compliance: Safeguarding Your Digital Assets

As organizations increasingly migrate their workloads and data to the cloud, ensuring cloud security and compliance becomes paramount. The cloud offers unparalleled flexibility and scalability, but it also introduces new challenges related to data protection, privacy, and regulatory requirements. In this in-depth exploration, we will delve into the strategies, best practices, and tools that organizations can leverage to secure their cloud environments and maintain compliance with relevant regulations.

1. Identity and Access Management (IAM):

1.1. Role-Based Access Control (RBAC):

- **IAM Policies:** Define and enforce IAM policies to ensure that users and services have the appropriate permissions based on their roles.

- **Least Privilege:** Follow the principle of least privilege to grant only the necessary permissions to perform specific tasks.

1.2. Multi-Factor Authentication (MFA):

- **MFA Implementation:** Require MFA for accessing sensitive resources and systems to enhance authentication security.

2. Data Encryption:

2.1. Data in Transit:

- **Transport Layer Security (TLS):** Use TLS encryption for data transmission between clients and cloud services to protect data in transit.

2.2. Data at Rest:

- **Encryption at Rest:** Implement encryption at rest for data stored in cloud storage services, databases, and backups.

3. Network Security:

3.1. Virtual Private Clouds (VPCs) and Virtual Networks (VNets):

- **Isolation:** Use VPCs or VNets to isolate network resources and control inbound and outbound traffic.

3.2. Network Security Groups (NSGs) and Firewalls:

- **NSGs and Firewalls:** Configure NSGs and firewalls to filter traffic and enforce network security policies.

4. Cloud Compliance:

4.1. Regulatory Compliance:

- **Understand Regulations:** Familiarize yourself with relevant regulations, such as GDPR, HIPAA, or PCI DSS, that apply to your industry or geography.

- **Compliance Tools:** Leverage compliance management tools and services provided by cloud providers or third-party solutions.

4.2. Compliance Controls:

- **Control Frameworks:** Implement control frameworks, such as the Center for Internet Security (CIS) benchmarks or the NIST Cybersecurity Framework, to guide compliance efforts.

5. Security Monitoring and Incident Response:

5.1. Security Information and Event Management (SIEM):

- **SIEM Solutions:** Deploy SIEM solutions to centralize the collection and analysis of security events and logs from cloud services.

5.2. Incident Response Plan:

- **Incident Response Plan:** Develop and regularly test an incident response plan to address security incidents promptly and effectively.

6. Data Privacy:

6.1. Data Classification:

- **Data Classification:** Categorize data based on sensitivity and apply appropriate security controls.

6.2. Data Residency:

- **Data Residency:** Understand where your data is stored and processed to ensure compliance with data privacy regulations.

7. Cloud Security Best Practices:

7.1. Security Training:

- **Employee Training:** Provide security training and awareness programs for employees to recognize and respond to security threats.

7.2. Continuous Security Assessment:

- **Vulnerability Scanning:** Regularly scan for vulnerabilities in cloud resources and applications.

- **Penetration Testing:** Conduct penetration testing to identify and remediate security weaknesses.

8. Compliance Audits:

8.1. Compliance Auditing:

- **Third-Party Audits:** Engage third-party auditors to perform compliance audits and assessments.

8.2. Compliance Reports:

- **Compliance Reports:** Obtain compliance reports and certifications from cloud providers to demonstrate adherence to security standards.

Securing cloud environments and maintaining compliance are ongoing efforts that require vigilance, monitoring, and adaptation as threats and regulations evolve. By implementing these strategies, best practices, and tools, organizations can effectively protect their digital assets in the cloud, maintain compliance with relevant regulations, and build trust with their customers and partners.

CHAPTER 10

Storage and Data Management: Navigating the Digital Data Seas

In today's data-driven world, organizations are inundated with vast volumes of data, ranging from customer information to operational records and beyond. Effectively managing, storing, and harnessing this data is crucial for business success. Storage and data management represent the cornerstone of modern IT infrastructure, providing the foundation upon which data-driven decisions, analytics, and innovation are built.

In this introductory exploration, we embark on a journey through the realms of storage and data management, where we will delve deep into the principles, technologies, and best practices that enable organizations to unlock the full potential of their data assets. From storage architectures and data backup strategies to data governance and analytics, we will navigate the digital data seas, equipping you with the knowledge and tools to harness the power of data for strategic advantage.

As we embark on this voyage, we will unravel the complexities of storage technologies, uncover the secrets of data protection, delve into the intricacies of data lifecycle management, and explore the transformative potential of big data and analytics.

Whether you are a seasoned IT professional seeking to optimize data infrastructure or a newcomer eager to dive into the world of data management, our journey into storage and data management promises to be both enlightening and empowering. So, hoist the sails, and let's navigate the digital data seas together.

A. Data Storage Technologies (SAN, NAS, Object Storage): Building the Foundation of Data Management

Data storage is the backbone of modern computing, enabling organizations to store, manage, and retrieve vast volumes of data efficiently and securely. Three fundamental data storage technologies—Storage Area Network (SAN), Network-Attached Storage (NAS), and Object Storage—form the core of data management strategies. In this in-depth exploration, we will dissect each of these technologies, unraveling their characteristics, use cases, and advantages in the world of data storage.

1. Storage Area Network (SAN):

1.1. Core Concept:

- **Block-Level Storage:** SAN is a high-speed, dedicated network that connects storage devices, such as disk arrays or storage arrays, to servers. It presents storage as block-level data, allowing servers to access storage devices as if they were directly attached.

1.2. Key Features:

- **High Performance:** SANs are designed for high-speed data transfer and low-latency access, making them suitable for mission-critical applications.

- **Scalability:** SANs can be easily scaled by adding more storage devices or upgrading existing ones.

1.3. Use Cases:

- **Database Hosting:** SANs are ideal for database servers that require high-performance storage with low latency.

- **Virtualization:** SANs support virtual machine storage for hypervisors like VMware or Hyper-V.

2. Network-Attached Storage (NAS):

2.1. Core Concept:

- **File-Level Storage:** NAS is a storage solution that provides file-level access to data over a network. It uses standard network protocols, such as NFS (Network File System) and SMB (Server Message Block).

2.2. Key Features:

- **Simplicity:** NAS is easy to set up and manage, making it suitable for file sharing and data access.

- **Scalability:** NAS devices can be expanded with additional drives or clustered to accommodate growing storage needs.

2.3. Use Cases:

- **File Sharing:** NAS is commonly used for file sharing among users or departments.

- **Backup and Archiving:** NAS devices are often used for data backup and archiving.

3. Object Storage:

3.1. Core Concept:

- **Object-Based Storage:** Object storage is a data storage architecture that manages data as objects rather than files or blocks. Each object consists of data, metadata, and a unique identifier.

3.2. Key Features:

- **Scalability:** Object storage systems are highly scalable, making them suitable for storing vast amounts of unstructured data.

- **Durability:** Object storage systems typically replicate data across multiple locations for high durability and availability.

3.3. Use Cases:

- **Big Data and Analytics:** Object storage is ideal for storing data used in big data analytics, machine learning, and data lakes.

- **Cloud Storage:** Many cloud providers use object storage to offer scalable and cost-effective storage services.

Choosing the Right Storage Technology:

- **Performance Requirements:** Consider the performance needs of your applications. SANs provide high performance, while NAS and object storage are better suited for applications with lower performance requirements.

- **Data Access Pattern:** Choose the technology that aligns with your data access pattern. Block-level SAN is suitable for databases, while NAS is ideal for file sharing and object storage for unstructured data.

- **Scalability:** Evaluate scalability requirements, as each technology has its scalability limits.

- **Cost:** Consider the total cost of ownership, including hardware, software, and management costs, when selecting a storage solution.

Data storage technologies, whether SAN, NAS, or object

storage, play a pivotal role in shaping an organization's data management strategy. By understanding the characteristics and best use cases of each technology, organizations can make informed decisions to build a robust and efficient data storage infrastructure that meets their specific business needs.

B. Data Backup and Recovery: Safeguarding Business Continuity

Data is the lifeblood of modern organizations, and the loss of critical data can be catastrophic. Data backup and recovery are essential components of an organization's data management strategy, ensuring the protection, availability, and resilience of data in the face of disasters, hardware failures, or human errors. In this in-depth exploration, we will delve into the principles, strategies, and best practices that underpin effective data backup and recovery.

1. Data Backup:

1.1. Backup Types:

- **Full Backup:** A full backup copies all data in a given dataset, providing a complete snapshot of the data at a specific point in time.

- **Incremental Backup:** Incremental backups capture only the changes made since the last backup, reducing storage requirements and backup time.

- **Differential Backup:** Differential backups store all changes made since the last full backup, making it faster to restore than incremental backups.

1.2. Backup Methods:

- **On-Premises Backup:** Traditional backup methods involve on-site storage solutions like tape drives, disk arrays, or backup servers.

- **Cloud Backup:** Cloud-based backup services offer scalable and cost-effective storage options for backup data.

2. Data Recovery:

2.1. Recovery Time Objective (RTO):

- **RTO:** RTO defines the maximum acceptable downtime for systems and applications. It influences the choice of recovery strategies.

2.2. Recovery Point Objective (RPO):

- **RPO:** RPO determines the acceptable data loss in case of a disaster. It helps decide backup frequency and retention policies.

3. Backup Storage:

3.1. Tape Storage:

- **Tape Backup:** Tape libraries and cartridges provide a cost-effective and offline backup storage option for long-term retention.

3.2. Disk Storage:

- **Disk Backup:** Disk-based storage offers fast backup and recovery times, making it suitable for frequent backups and quick restores.

3.3. Cloud Storage:

- **Cloud Backup:** Cloud storage services enable organizations to store backups off-site, providing scalability and accessibility.

4. Backup and Recovery Strategies:

4.1. 3-2-1 Backup Rule:

- **3-2-1 Rule:** Maintain three copies of data (original + two backups), store backups on two different media types, and keep one backup off-site.

4.2. Disaster Recovery Plan:

- **Disaster Recovery (DR) Plan:** Develop a comprehensive DR plan that outlines procedures for data recovery and system restoration.

4.3. Backup Testing:

- **Backup Testing:** Regularly test backups to ensure data integrity and verify that recovery processes work as expected.

5. Data Encryption:

5.1. Backup Encryption:

- **Backup Encryption:** Encrypt backup data to protect it from unauthorized access during storage and transmission.

6. Backup Automation:

6.1. Backup Software:

- **Backup Software:** Use backup software to automate backup processes, schedule backups, and manage backup policies.

6.2. Orchestration:

- **Orchestration:** Implement orchestration tools to automate and streamline complex backup and recovery workflows.

7. Backup Retention:

7.1. Data Lifecycle Management:

- **Data Lifecycle Management:** Define data retention policies based on legal requirements and business needs.

8. Monitoring and Alerts:

8.1. Backup Monitoring:

- **Backup Monitoring:** Implement monitoring tools to continuously track backup jobs, storage utilization, and potential issues.

8.2. Alerting:

- **Alerting:** Set up alerts to notify administrators of backup failures or anomalies.

9. Cloud-Based Disaster Recovery:

9.1. Disaster Recovery as a Service (DRaaS):

- **DRaaS:** Consider DRaaS solutions that provide automated failover to cloud environments in case of a disaster.

Data backup and recovery are foundational elements of a robust data management strategy. By implementing effective backup practices, organizations can safeguard their data against loss or corruption and ensure business continuity even in the face of unforeseen challenges. A well-planned and regularly tested backup and recovery strategy provides the peace of mind needed to navigate the data-driven landscape with confidence.

C. Data Lifecycle Management: Maximizing the Value of Data from Birth to Retirement

Data is a valuable asset for organizations, but managing it throughout its lifecycle is a complex endeavor. Data Lifecycle Management (DLM) is a structured approach to the management of data from its creation or acquisition to its deletion or archival. DLM encompasses data storage, retention, preservation, and disposal, with the overarching goal of maximizing the value of data while ensuring compliance, security, and efficiency. In this in-depth exploration, we will journey through the stages of data lifecycle management, uncovering strategies, best practices, and the significance of each phase.

1. Data Creation and Ingestion:

1.1. Data Sources:

- **Data Sources:** Data is generated from various sources, including applications, sensors, user inputs, and external datasets.

1.2. Data Ingestion:

- **Data Ingestion:** Ingest data into the organization's systems, databases, or data lakes for further processing.

2. Data Classification:

2.1. Data Categorization:

- **Data Categorization:** Classify data based on its sensitivity, importance, and relevance to the organization.

2.2. Metadata:

- **Metadata:** Create and maintain metadata to provide context and information about the data's characteristics and usage.

3. Data Storage and Access:

3.1. Storage Infrastructure:

- **Storage Infrastructure:** Store data in appropriate storage solutions, such as databases, file systems, cloud storage, or data warehouses.

3.2. Access Control:

- **Access Control:** Implement access controls to restrict data access based on roles and permissions.

4. Data Usage and Analysis:

4.1. Data Analytics:

- **Data Analytics:** Utilize data for various purposes, including business intelligence, reporting, and machine learning.

4.2. Data Transformation:

- **Data Transformation:** Prepare and transform data to make it suitable for analysis and reporting.

5. Data Retention and Archival:

5.1. Retention Policies:

- **Data Retention Policies:** Define policies that specify how long data should be retained based on regulatory requirements and business needs.

5.2. Archiving:

- **Data Archiving:** Move less frequently accessed data to archival storage to free up primary storage resources.

6. Data Deletion:

6.1. Data Purge:

- **Data Purge:** Permanently delete data that is no longer needed or has reached the end of its retention period.

7. Data Backup and Recovery:

7.1. Backup:

- **Data Backup:** Regularly back up critical data to ensure data availability and disaster recovery.

7.2. Recovery:

- **Data Recovery:** Implement processes and solutions for data recovery in case of data loss or disasters.

8. Data Security:

8.1. Data Encryption:

- **Data Encryption:** Protect data at rest and in transit through encryption to mitigate data breaches.

8.2. Data Masking:

- **Data Masking:** Anonymize or mask sensitive data to ensure privacy and compliance.

9. Data Auditing and Compliance:

9.1. Data Audits:

- **Data Auditing:** Conduct regular data audits to ensure compliance with regulations and internal policies.

9.2. Compliance Reporting:

- **Compliance Reporting:** Generate compliance reports and maintain records to demonstrate adherence to data regulations.

10. Data Disposal and Destruction:

10.1. Secure Data Destruction:

- **Secure Data Destruction:** Use secure methods to permanently delete data, including physical destruction of storage media.

10.2. Records of Destruction:

- **Records of Destruction:** Maintain records of data destruction activities for compliance and auditing purposes.

Effective Data Lifecycle Management ensures that data remains a valuable asset throughout its existence. By understanding and implementing strategies and best practices for each stage of the data lifecycle, organizations can derive meaningful insights from their data, enhance data security and compliance, optimize storage costs, and maintain a competitive edge in the data-driven landscape.

D. Big Data and Analytics Infrastructure: Fueling Data-Driven Insights

In today's data-driven world, organizations are inundated with vast volumes of data from a myriad of sources. To gain valuable insights, they rely on Big Data and Analytics Infrastructure—an ecosystem of technologies, tools, and practices designed to capture, store, process, and analyze large and complex datasets. In this in-depth exploration, we will dissect the components, challenges, and advantages of Big Data and Analytics Infrastructure, uncovering how it fuels data-driven decision-making and innovation.

1. The Big Data Challenge:

1.1. Data Volume:

- **Data Volume:** Big data refers to datasets that are too large to be handled by traditional data processing tools. These datasets can range from terabytes to petabytes or more.

1.2. Data Variety:

- **Data Variety:** Big data encompasses structured, semi-structured, and unstructured data, including text, images, videos, and sensor data.

1.3. Data Velocity:

- **Data Velocity:** Big data often arrives at high speeds, requiring real-time or near-real-time processing and analysis.

2. Big Data Technologies:

2.1. Data Storage:

- **Distributed File Systems:** Technologies like Hadoop Distributed File System (HDFS) and Amazon S3 store and manage large datasets across multiple nodes.

2.2. Data Processing:

- **MapReduce:** A programming model for processing and generating large datasets that parallelizes the computation.

- **Apache Spark:** An open-source data processing framework that provides in-memory processing and data streaming capabilities.

2.3. Data Query and Analysis:

- **NoSQL Databases:** NoSQL databases, like MongoDB and Cassandra, are designed for handling unstructured and semi-structured data.

- **SQL-on-Hadoop:** Tools like Apache Hive and Impala enable SQL-like querying on big data stored in Hadoop.

2.4. Data Streaming:

- **Stream Processing:** Technologies like Apache Kafka and Apache Flink enable real-time processing of data streams.

3. Analytics Infrastructure:

3.1. Data Warehousing:

- **Data Warehouses:** These store structured data and support complex querying for business intelligence and reporting.

- **Cloud Data Warehouses:** Services like Amazon Redshift and Google BigQuery offer scalable, cloud-based data warehousing solutions.

3.2. Business Intelligence (BI) Tools:

- **BI Tools:** Tools like Tableau, Power BI, and QlikView enable users to visualize and explore data for insights.

3.3. Machine Learning (ML) and Artificial Intelligence (AI):

- **ML and AI Platforms:** Platforms like TensorFlow and scikit-learn provide tools for developing and deploying machine learning models.

4. Challenges and Considerations:

4.1. Data Security and Privacy:

- **Data Security:** Big data environments require robust security measures to protect sensitive data.

- **Data Privacy:** Compliance with data privacy regulations, such as GDPR, is crucial.

4.2. Scalability:

- **Scalability:** As data grows, infrastructure must scale seamlessly to accommodate increased storage and processing demands.

4.3. Data Quality:

- **Data Quality:** Ensuring data accuracy and consistency is challenging with large and diverse datasets.

4.4. Talent and Skillsets:

- **Data Expertise:** Organizations need skilled data professionals, including data scientists and engineers.

5. Benefits of Big Data and Analytics Infrastructure:

5.1. Data-Driven Insights:

- **Data-Driven Decisions:** Organizations can make informed decisions based on data-driven insights.

5.2. Competitive Advantage:

- **Competitive Edge:** Leveraging big data analytics can lead to a competitive advantage by identifying trends and opportunities.

5.3. Innovation:

- **Innovation:** Big data fosters innovation by enabling the development of new products and services.

5.4. Operational Efficiency:

- **Operational Efficiency:** Analyzing data can optimize processes, reduce costs, and improve overall efficiency.

6. Future Trends:

6.1. Edge Computing:

- **Edge Computing:** Analyzing data closer to its source (at the edge) for real-time processing.

6.2. AI and Machine Learning:

- **AI and ML Integration:** Greater integration of AI and ML into big data analytics for predictive insights.

Big Data and Analytics Infrastructure have transformed the way organizations operate and make decisions. By harnessing the power of big data technologies and analytics tools, organizations can extract valuable insights, uncover hidden patterns, and drive innovation in an increasingly data-centric world. As data continues to grow in volume and complexity, the role of Big Data and Analytics Infrastructure in shaping the future of businesses becomes even more critical.

E. Data Governance and Compliance: Upholding Data Integrity and Legal Standards

Data is a valuable asset for organizations, but its management and protection are governed by a complex web of regulations and internal policies. Data Governance and Compliance are essential components of an organization's data management strategy, ensuring that data is used, stored, and shared in a manner that adheres to legal and regulatory requirements while maintaining its quality and integrity. In this in-depth exploration, we will dissect the principles, challenges, and best practices that underpin effective Data Governance and Compliance.

1. Data Governance:

1.1. Definition:

- **Data Governance:** Data Governance is the framework of policies, processes, and roles responsible for managing, protecting, and ensuring the quality and integrity of data.

1.2. Key Components:

- **Data Stewardship:** Assigning data stewards responsible for data quality and compliance.

- **Data Policies:** Establishing policies for data access, usage, and security.

- **Data Quality:** Ensuring data accuracy, consistency, and reliability.

1.3. Benefits:

- **Data Consistency:** Data Governance ensures consistent data definitions and standards across the organization.

- **Compliance:** It helps organizations adhere to regulatory requirements.

2. Regulatory Compliance:

2.1. Data Protection Regulations:

- **GDPR:** The General Data Protection Regulation (GDPR) governs the privacy and protection of personal data in the European Union.

- **HIPAA:** The Health Insurance Portability and Accountability Act (HIPAA) sets standards for protecting health information.

2.2. Industry-Specific Regulations:

- **PCI DSS:** The Payment Card Industry Data Security Standard (PCI DSS) applies to organizations that handle credit card information.

- **FERPA:** The Family Educational Rights and Privacy Act (FERPA) governs the privacy of student records.

3. Data Classification:

3.1. Data Sensitivity:

- **Data Sensitivity:** Classify data based on its sensitivity level to determine access controls.

3.2. Data Labels:

- **Data Labels:** Use data labels to indicate the sensitivity and handling requirements of data.

4. Data Access Control:

4.1. Role-Based Access Control (RBAC):

- **RBAC:** Assign data access rights based on roles and responsibilities.

4.2. Data Encryption:

- **Data Encryption:** Encrypt sensitive data to protect it from unauthorized access.

5. Data Auditing and Monitoring:

5.1. Audit Trails:

- **Audit Trails:** Maintain audit trails to track data access and changes.

5.2. Security Information and Event Management (SIEM):

- **SIEM:** Use SIEM systems to monitor and detect security events and incidents.

6. Data Privacy:

6.1. Consent Management:

- **Consent Management:** Implement processes for obtaining and managing user consent for data processing.

6.2. Data Subject Rights:

- **Data Subject Rights:** Ensure compliance with regulations that grant individuals rights over their data, such as the right to be forgotten.

7. Data Retention and Deletion:

7.1. Data Retention Policies:

- **Data Retention Policies:** Define how long data should be retained based on regulatory requirements and business needs.

7.2. Data Deletion:

- **Data Deletion:** Establish procedures for permanently deleting data that is no longer needed.

8. Data Governance Framework:

8.1. Data Governance Committee:

- **Data Governance Committee:** Form a committee responsible for overseeing data governance activities.

8.2. Data Governance Charter:

- **Data Governance Charter:** Create a charter that outlines the organization's data governance principles, roles, and responsibilities.

Effective Data Governance and Compliance are essential for maintaining trust with customers, partners, and regulators while harnessing the value of data. Organizations that implement robust governance frameworks and adhere to compliance standards not only mitigate legal and reputational risks but also foster a culture of data responsibility and accountability. In a world where data is a strategic asset, Data Governance and Compliance play a pivotal role in shaping how organizations manage, protect, and leverage their data.

CHAPTER 11

Virtualization and Containerization: Unleashing the Power of Resource Efficiency

Virtualization and containerization are transformative technologies that have revolutionized the world of IT infrastructure and software deployment. They offer innovative approaches to optimizing resource utilization, enhancing scalability, and streamlining application deployment. In this introductory exploration, we will embark on a journey to understand the fundamental concepts of virtualization and containerization, unraveling their significance in modern computing.

1. Virtualization:

1.1. Definition:

- **Virtualization:** Virtualization is the process of creating a virtual representation of physical resources, such as servers, storage, or networks. It allows multiple virtual instances or machines to run on a single physical host.

1.2. Key Components:

- **Hypervisor:** A hypervisor, also known as a virtual machine

299

monitor (VMM), is the software or hardware that manages and allocates physical resources to virtual machines (VMs).

- **Virtual Machines:** VMs are isolated, independent instances of operating systems and applications that run on a single physical host.

1.3. Benefits:

- **Resource Utilization:** Virtualization optimizes hardware utilization, enabling multiple workloads to share the same physical infrastructure.

- **Isolation:** VMs provide isolation, ensuring that issues in one VM do not affect others.

2. Containerization:

2.1. Definition:

- **Containerization:** Containerization is a lightweight form of virtualization that encapsulates applications and their dependencies into self-contained units called containers.

2.2. Key Components:

- **Containers:** Containers package an application and its dependencies, including libraries and configuration files, into a single unit.

- **Container Runtime:** Container runtimes, like Docker, provide the environment for running containers.

2.3. Benefits:

- **Efficiency:** Containers are highly efficient, as they share the host's operating system kernel and require fewer resources than VMs.

- **Portability:** Containers can run consistently across different environments, from development to production.

3. Use Cases:

3.1. Virtualization Use Cases:

- **Server Virtualization:** Consolidate multiple servers onto a single physical host.

- **Desktop Virtualization:** Run multiple virtual desktops on a single client machine.

3.2. Containerization Use Cases:

- **Microservices Architecture:** Deploy and manage microservices in separate containers for agility and scalability.

- **Continuous Integration/Continuous Deployment (CI/CD):** Use containers to ensure consistent environments for development and testing.

4. Container Orchestration:

4.1. Kubernetes:

- **Kubernetes:** Kubernetes is an open-source container orchestration platform that automates container deployment, scaling, and management.

4.2. Benefits of Orchestration:

- **Scalability:** Orchestration tools like Kubernetes enable automatic scaling of containerized applications.

- **Load Balancing:** They manage load balancing and service discovery.

Virtualization and containerization are pivotal technologies that have transformed how IT infrastructure is managed and how applications are deployed. Understanding these concepts and their applications is essential in the modern IT landscape, where resource efficiency, scalability, and agility are paramount. As we delve deeper into these technologies, we will uncover their intricate workings and explore how they have shaped the evolution of computing.

A. Virtualization Technologies: Unlocking Efficiency and Flexibility with VMware and Hyper-V

Virtualization technologies, exemplified by industry giants like VMware and Microsoft's Hyper-V, have reshaped the landscape of IT infrastructure and computing. These technologies provide the means to create virtual environments, enabling multiple operating systems and applications to run on a single physical host. In this in-depth exploration, we'll delve into VMware and Hyper-V, uncovering their core features, benefits, and their significant roles in modern IT ecosystems.

1. VMware:

1.1. Introduction to VMware:

- **VMware:** VMware, founded in 1998, is a global leader in virtualization and cloud infrastructure solutions. It offers a wide range of virtualization products and services for data centers, cloud environments, and endpoint devices.

1.2. Key Components of VMware:

- **Hypervisor:** VMware's ESXi hypervisor is at the core of its virtualization solutions, providing the foundation for virtual machine creation and management.

- **vCenter Server:** vCenter Server is a centralized management platform that simplifies the administration of virtualized environments, allowing administrators to control multiple ESXi hosts and VMs.

1.3. Benefits of VMware:

- **Resource Optimization:** VMware enables efficient utilization of hardware resources, reducing the need for additional physical servers.

- **High Availability:** Features like vMotion and Fault Tolerance ensure high availability and minimize downtime.

- **Disaster Recovery:** VMware Site Recovery Manager (SRM) automates the disaster recovery process.

2. Hyper-V:

2.1. Introduction to Hyper-V:

- **Hyper-V:** Microsoft Hyper-V, part of Windows Server, is a virtualization platform for creating and managing virtualized environments on Windows-based servers.

2.2. Key Components of Hyper-V:

- **Hyper-V Hypervisor:** Hyper-V's hypervisor is integrated into Windows Server and provides the foundation for virtualization.

- **Hyper-V Manager:** Hyper-V Manager is the primary tool for managing virtual machines and their configurations.

2.3. Benefits of Hyper-V:

- **Cost-Effective:** Hyper-V is often a cost-effective choice for organizations already invested in the Microsoft ecosystem.

- **Integration:** Tight integration with Windows and Active Directory simplifies management.

- **Live Migration:** Hyper-V offers Live Migration, allowing VMs to move between hosts with minimal downtime.

3. Feature Comparison:

3.1. Licensing:

- **VMware:** VMware typically requires separate licensing, and costs can vary based on the edition and features.

- **Hyper-V:** Hyper-V is included with Windows Server licensing, making it a cost-effective option for Windows-centric environments.

3.2. Ecosystem:

- **VMware:** VMware has a robust ecosystem with a wide range of products and solutions, including vSpherc, NSX for network virtualization, and vSAN for storage.

- **Hyper-V:** Hyper-V integrates seamlessly with Microsoft technologies, including System Center for management and Azure for cloud services.

3.3. Community and Support:

- **VMware:** VMware has a large user community and offers comprehensive support and training resources.

- **Hyper-V:** Hyper-V benefits from Microsoft's extensive support and documentation.

4. Use Cases:

4.1. VMware Use Cases:

- **Enterprise Data Centers:** VMware is widely used in large-scale data center environments for server consolidation and virtualization.

- **Cloud Environments:** VMware Cloud provides a platform for building and managing cloud infrastructure.

4.2. Hyper-V Use Cases:

- **Windows-Centric Environments:** Hyper-V is a natural choice for organizations heavily reliant on Windows-based servers.

- **Small to Medium-Sized Businesses (SMBs):** Hyper-V's cost-effectiveness makes it attractive to SMBs.

Virtualization technologies like VMware and Hyper-V have become indispensable in modern IT environments. They offer efficient resource utilization, scalability, and high availability, enabling organizations to adapt to changing business needs and streamline IT operations. By understanding the nuances and capabilities of these technologies, organizations can make informed decisions about their virtualization strategy and harness the full potential of their IT infrastructure.

B. Containerization: Revolutionizing Software Deployment with Docker and Kubernetes

Containerization has emerged as a transformative technology in the world of software development and deployment, offering a lightweight and portable solution for packaging applications and their dependencies. Docker and Kubernetes, two prominent containerization technologies, have played pivotal roles in reshaping how applications are built, shipped, and run. In this in-depth exploration, we will unravel the core concepts, benefits, and the critical roles Docker and Kubernetes play in modern IT ecosystems.

1. Docker:

1.1. Introduction to Docker:

- **Docker:** Docker is an open-source platform for developing, shipping, and running applications within containers. It was introduced in 2013 and has since gained widespread adoption in the software development community.

1.2. Key Components of Docker:

- **Docker Engine:** The Docker Engine is the core component responsible for creating and running containers. It includes the Docker daemon, which manages containers, and the Docker client, which interacts with the daemon.

- **Docker Hub:** Docker Hub is a cloud-based registry that stores Docker images, making it easy to share and distribute containerized applications.

1.3. Benefits of Docker:

- **Isolation:** Containers encapsulate applications and their dependencies, providing isolation from the host system and other containers.

- **Portability:** Docker containers can run consistently across different environments, from development to production.

- **Resource Efficiency:** Containers are lightweight and share the host's operating system kernel, minimizing resource overhead.

2. Kubernetes:

2.1. Introduction to Kubernetes:

- **Kubernetes:** Kubernetes, often abbreviated as K8s, is an open-source container orchestration platform introduced by Google. It automates the deployment, scaling, and management of containerized applications.

2.2. Key Components of Kubernetes:

- **Cluster:** A Kubernetes cluster comprises a set of physical or virtual machines (nodes) organized into a master node and worker nodes.

- **Pod:** A pod is the smallest deployable unit in Kubernetes and can contain one or more containers.

- **Service:** Kubernetes services enable network access to a set of pods, providing load balancing and DNS-based service discovery.

2.3. Benefits of Kubernetes:

- **Orchestration:** Kubernetes automates container deployment, scaling, and management, simplifying complex application architectures.

- **Scaling:** It supports horizontal scaling, allowing applications to handle varying workloads.

- **Self-healing:** Kubernetes can automatically replace failed containers or nodes, ensuring high availability.

3. Docker vs. Kubernetes:

3.1. Docker vs. Kubernetes Roles:

- **Docker:** Docker is primarily focused on container creation, packaging, and distribution.

- **Kubernetes:** Kubernetes is an orchestration platform that manages containerized applications' deployment and scaling.

3.2. Complementary Technologies:

- **Docker and Kubernetes:** Docker and Kubernetes are often used together, with Docker providing containerization, and Kubernetes handling orchestration and management.

4. Use Cases:

4.1. Docker Use Cases:

- **Local Development:** Developers use Docker to create development environments that match production.

- **Continuous Integration/Continuous Deployment (CI/CD):** Docker containers simplify the deployment process.

4.2. Kubernetes Use Cases:

- **Scalable Web Applications:** Kubernetes scales applications based on demand, making it suitable for web services.

- **Microservices:** Kubernetes excels at managing microservices-based architectures.

5. Community and Ecosystem:

- **Docker:** Docker has a large user community, and Docker Hub hosts a vast repository of container images.

- **Kubernetes:** Kubernetes has a thriving community and a rich ecosystem of tools and extensions.

Containerization technologies like Docker and Kubernetes have ushered in a new era of software development and deployment. They empower organizations to build, package, and deploy applications with unparalleled efficiency, scalability, and consistency. As the containerization landscape continues to evolve, staying informed about the latest advancements and best practices is essential for organizations looking to maximize the benefits of these transformative technologies.

C. Microservices Architecture: Building Scalable and Agile Software Ecosystems

Microservices architecture is a revolutionary approach to designing and building software applications that has gained immense popularity in recent years. It breaks down monolithic applications into smaller, independently deployable services, each responsible for a specific business function. This in-depth exploration delves into the core concepts, advantages, challenges, and best practices of microservices architecture, shedding light on its pivotal role in modern software development.

1. Introduction to Microservices:

1.1. Definition:

- **Microservices:** Microservices is an architectural style where an application is composed of loosely coupled, independently deployable services that collaborate to provide the application's overall functionality.

1.2. Key Characteristics:

- **Decomposition:** Applications are divided into small, focused services that can be developed, deployed, and scaled independently.

- **Independence:** Each microservice has its own database and can use different technologies, enabling teams to choose the most suitable tools for their service.

1.3. Advantages:

- **Scalability:** Microservices can be scaled individually, allowing efficient resource utilization.

- **Agility:** Teams can work on different services simultaneously, accelerating development cycles.

- **Resilience:** Isolated services can fail without affecting the entire application.

2. Microservices Communication:

2.1. Communication Protocols:

- **RESTful APIs:** Representational State Transfer (REST) APIs are commonly used for communication between microservices.

- **gRPC:** A high-performance RPC (Remote Procedure Call) framework developed by Google.

2.2. Service Discovery:

- **Service Registry:** Tools like Consul or Eureka help services discover and communicate with each other.

3. Data Management:

3.1. Polyglot Persistence:

- **Polyglot Persistence:** Microservices can use different databases (SQL, NoSQL) based on the specific requirements of each service.

3.2. Event Sourcing and CQRS:

- **Event Sourcing:** Storing the state of an application as a sequence of events.

- **CQRS (Command Query Responsibility Segregation):** Separating the command (write) and query (read) responsibilities in the system.

4. Challenges of Microservices:

4.1. Complexity: Managing a distributed system can be complex, especially in terms of deployment and monitoring.

4.2. Data Consistency: Ensuring data consistency across services can be challenging due to the distributed nature of microservices.

4.3. Service Coordination: Coordinating actions across services, such as transactions, can be complex.

5. Best Practices:

5.1. Independent Deployment: Each service should be independently deployable.

5.2. Continuous Integration/Continuous Deployment (CI/CD): Implement CI/CD pipelines to automate testing and deployment.

5.3. Monitoring and Observability: Use tools like Prometheus and Grafana to monitor the health and performance of services.

5.4. Service Resilience: Implement retry mechanisms and circuit breakers to handle service failures gracefully.

6. Use Cases:

6.1. E-commerce: Microservices enable flexible and scalable e-commerce platforms with services for product catalog, checkout, payment processing, and more.

6.2. Social Media: Social media platforms can use microservices to handle user profiles, feeds, notifications, and messaging.

7. Industry Adoption:

- **Netflix:** Netflix migrated from a monolithic architecture to microservices, improving scalability and availability.

- **Uber:** Uber's microservices-based architecture powers its ride-sharing platform.

Microservices architecture is a powerful approach for building software systems that are agile, scalable, and resilient. While it offers numerous advantages, it also presents challenges that organizations must address to fully realize its benefits. As the software development landscape continues to evolve, microservices are expected to remain a cornerstone of modern application architecture, shaping how businesses create and deliver software solutions.

D. Orchestrating Containers: Streamlining Deployment and Management with Kubernetes

Orchestrating containers is a critical aspect of modern software deployment, enabling organizations to efficiently manage large-scale containerized applications. Kubernetes, the leading container orchestration platform, has emerged as the go-to solution for automating the deployment, scaling, and management of containerized workloads. In this in-depth exploration, we will delve into the principles, components, benefits, and best practices of orchestrating containers with Kubernetes.

1. Container Orchestration:

1.1. Definition:

- **Container Orchestration:** Container orchestration is the automated management of containerized applications, including tasks such as deployment, scaling, load balancing, and service discovery.

1.2. Key Objectives:

- **Efficient Resource Utilization:** Orchestration ensures that containers are deployed on appropriate nodes, optimizing resource allocation.

- **High Availability:** Orchestration platforms monitor container health and automatically replace failed containers or nodes.

2. Introduction to Kubernetes:

2.1. Kubernetes Overview:

- **Kubernetes:** Kubernetes, often abbreviated as K8s, is an open-source container orchestration platform initially developed by Google and now managed by the Cloud Native Computing Foundation (CNCF).

2.2. Key Kubernetes Components:

- **Cluster:** A Kubernetes cluster consists of a master node that controls worker nodes where containers run.

- **Pod:** A pod is the smallest deployable unit in Kubernetes and can contain one or more containers.

- **ReplicaSet:** ReplicaSets ensure that a specified number of pod replicas are running at any given time.

- **Service:** Kubernetes services provide network access to a set of pods, enabling load balancing and service discovery.

3. Benefits of Kubernetes:

3.1. Scalability:

- **Horizontal Scaling:** Kubernetes scales applications by adding or removing pod replicas based on demand.

- **Vertical Scaling:** Vertical Pod Autoscaler adjusts CPU and memory resource requests for pods.

3.2. High Availability:

- **Self-Healing:** Kubernetes detects and replaces failed containers or nodes to maintain application availability.

- **Multi-Region Deployments:** Kubernetes supports multi-region deployments for enhanced availability.

3.3. Portability:

- **Hybrid and Multi-Cloud:** Kubernetes provides portability across different cloud providers and on-premises environments.

4. Kubernetes Resources:

4.1. Configuration Files:

- **YAML Files:** Kubernetes resources, such as pods and services, are defined in YAML configuration files.

4.2. Deployment:

- **Deployment:** A Kubernetes resource that manages the desired state of replica sets, ensuring that the specified number of pod replicas are running.

4.3. StatefulSet:

- **StatefulSet:** Used for managing stateful applications that require stable network identities and persistent storage.

5. Deployment Strategies:

5.1. Blue-Green Deployment:

- **Blue-Green Deployment:** Involves running two identical environments (blue and green) with one live and the other inactive, facilitating seamless updates.

5.2. Canary Deployment:

- **Canary Deployment:** Gradually rolls out changes to a subset of users or traffic before deploying to the entire application.

6. Monitoring and Logging:

- Kubernetes integrates with monitoring and logging solutions like Prometheus and Elasticsearch for tracking container and cluster health.

7. Use Cases:

7.1. Microservices-Based Applications: Kubernetes is well-suited for managing microservices-based applications with multiple interconnected services.

7.2. Continuous Integration/Continuous Deployment (CI/CD): Kubernetes integrates seamlessly with CI/CD pipelines for automated application deployment.

8. Best Practices:

8.1. Infrastructure as Code (IaC):

- Define Kubernetes resources using Infrastructure as Code principles for reproducibility and version control.

8.2. Resource Requests and Limits:

- Specify resource requests and limits for containers to ensure efficient resource utilization.

8.3. Rolling Updates and Rollbacks:

- Plan and test rolling updates and rollbacks to minimize service disruption.

Kubernetes has become the de facto standard for container orchestration due to its robust feature set, extensibility, and large user community. As organizations continue to adopt containerization and microservices, Kubernetes plays a pivotal role in managing complex containerized applications efficiently. Understanding the principles and best practices of orchestrating containers with Kubernetes is essential for achieving seamless and scalable deployments in the modern IT landscape.

E. Container Security and Management: Safeguarding Containerized Applications

Containerization has revolutionized software deployment by offering lightweight, portable, and scalable solutions. However, with great flexibility comes a significant responsibility for security and management. In this in-depth exploration, we will delve into the critical aspects of container security and management, examining best practices, tools, and strategies to ensure the safety and efficiency of containerized applications.

1. Container Security:

1.1. Image Security:

- **Vulnerability Scanning:** Tools like Clair, Trivy, and Anchore scan container images for known vulnerabilities and issues.

- **Image Signing:** Digitally sign container images to verify their authenticity and integrity.

1.2. Runtime Security:

- **Isolation:** Ensure containers are isolated from the host and other containers to prevent unauthorized access.

- **AppArmor and Seccomp:** Use security profiles like AppArmor and Seccomp to restrict container processes.

1.3. Network Security:

- **Network Policies:** Kubernetes Network Policies define rules for network communication between pods.

- **Service Mesh:** Implement service mesh technologies like Istio or Linkerd for enhanced network security and observability.

1.4. Compliance and Auditing:

- **Container Security Standards:** Adhere to container security standards like CIS Docker Benchmark.

- **Audit Logs:** Enable and monitor container audit logs to detect and investigate security incidents.

2. Container Management:

2.1. Orchestration:

- **Kubernetes:** Kubernetes orchestrates containerized applications, managing deployment, scaling, and load balancing.

- **Docker Swarm:** Docker Swarm provides built-in orchestration capabilities for Docker containers.

2.2. Configuration Management:

- **Infrastructure as Code (IaC):** Use IaC tools like Terraform or Ansible to define and manage container infrastructure.

- **Configuration Files:** Define container configurations in YAML or JSON files for reproducibility.

2.3. Monitoring and Logging:

- **Prometheus and Grafana:** Implement monitoring and alerting with tools like Prometheus and Grafana to track container health.

- **Elasticsearch and Kibana:** Centralize container logs with Elasticsearch and visualize data with Kibana.

2.4. Continuous Integration/Continuous Deployment (CI/CD):

- **CI/CD Pipelines:** Implement CI/CD pipelines to automate container image building, testing, and deployment.

- **GitOps:** Embrace GitOps practices for declarative and version-controlled container management.

3. Container Registries:

3.1. Docker Hub:

- **Docker Hub:** Docker Hub is a public container registry for sharing and distributing container images.

3.2. Private Registries:

- **Private Registries:** Organizations often use private container registries like Amazon ECR, Google Container Registry (GCR), or Azure Container Registry (ACR) to store proprietary images.

4. Best Practices:

4.1. Least Privilege Principle:

- Apply the principle of least privilege, ensuring containers have only the necessary permissions and access.

4.2. Immutable Infrastructure:

- Treat containers as immutable, rebuilding them from scratch for each change to minimize vulnerabilities.

4.3. Patch Management:

- Regularly update and patch container images to address security vulnerabilities.

4.4. Disaster Recovery:

- Implement disaster recovery plans for containerized applications to ensure business continuity.

5. Use Cases:

5.1. Microservices-Based Applications:

- Containerization and orchestration are ideal for managing complex microservices architectures.

5.2. Multi-Cloud Deployments:

- Containers enable consistent application deployment across multiple cloud providers.

Container security and management are fundamental considerations in the containerization journey. By implementing robust security practices, orchestration, and management strategies, organizations can harness the full potential of containerized applications while mitigating security risks and ensuring operational efficiency in today's dynamic software landscape.

CHAPTER 12

Advanced Security Measures: Fortifying Your Digital Defenses

In an era of ever-evolving cyber threats and sophisticated attack vectors, advanced security measures have become paramount in safeguarding digital assets, privacy, and critical infrastructure. This introductory exploration delves into the realm of advanced security measures, encompassing cutting-edge technologies, strategies, and practices designed to protect organizations and individuals from the most sophisticated cyber threats in the digital landscape.

A. Intrusion Detection Systems (IDS): Fortifying Your Digital Perimeter

Intrusion Detection Systems (IDS) are a critical component of modern cybersecurity, serving as vigilant sentinels that monitor network traffic and system behavior for signs of unauthorized access, suspicious activities, or security breaches. In this in-depth exploration, we will delve into the world of Intrusion Detection Systems, examining their types, functioning, benefits, and the pivotal role they play in safeguarding digital assets and networks.

1. Introduction to Intrusion Detection Systems:

1.1. Definition:

- **Intrusion Detection System (IDS):** An IDS is a cybersecurity technology designed to detect and alert on anomalous or malicious activities within a network or system.

1.2. Key Objectives:

- **Threat Detection:** IDS identifies potential security incidents and threats, including unauthorized access, malware infections, and suspicious traffic patterns.

- **Real-time Monitoring:** It provides real-time or near-real-time alerts, allowing rapid response to security incidents.

2. Types of Intrusion Detection Systems:

2.1. Network-Based IDS (NIDS):

- **NIDS:** Network-Based IDS monitors network traffic and identifies suspicious patterns or signatures that may indicate an attack.

2.2. Host-Based IDS (HIDS):

- **HIDS:** Host-Based IDS focuses on individual host systems, analyzing log files and system activities to detect intrusions.

2.3. Behavior-Based IDS:

- **Behavior-Based IDS:** These systems establish a baseline of normal system or network behavior and alert on deviations from this baseline.

2.4. Signature-Based IDS:

- **Signature-Based IDS:** These IDS use predefined signatures or patterns to identify known threats.

3. How IDS Works:

3.1. Data Collection:

- IDS collects data from network traffic, system logs, or system activities.

3.2. Analysis:

- It analyzes the collected data using various methods, including signature matching, anomaly detection, and heuristics.

3.3. Alerting:

- When suspicious activity is detected, the IDS generates alerts or notifications for security administrators or systems.

4. Benefits of IDS:

4.1. Early Threat Detection:

- IDS detects threats at an early stage, minimizing the potential impact of security incidents.

4.2. Real-time Alerts:

- It provides real-time alerts, allowing security teams to respond promptly to security breaches.

4.3. Compliance:

- IDS helps organizations comply with regulatory requirements by monitoring and reporting on security events.

5. Challenges of IDS:

5.1. False Positives:

- IDS may generate false positives, where benign activities are mistaken for threats.

5.2. Evading Detection:

- Sophisticated attackers can craft attacks to bypass signature-based IDS.

5.3. Volume of Data:

- The sheer volume of network traffic and system logs can overwhelm IDS, making it challenging to detect subtle anomalies.

6. Intrusion Prevention Systems (IPS):

- Intrusion Prevention Systems (IPS) go a step further by not only detecting but also actively preventing detected threats. IPS can automatically block or contain malicious traffic.

7. Use Cases:

7.1. Network Security:

- IDS is a crucial component of network security, helping protect networks from unauthorized access, data breaches, and cyberattacks.

7.2. Server Security:

- HIDS is commonly used to monitor server activities and detect unauthorized changes or access.

8. Emerging Trends:

- AI and Machine Learning: IDS systems are increasingly incorporating AI and machine learning algorithms to improve threat detection accuracy.

- Cloud-Based IDS: With the rise of cloud computing, cloud-based IDS solutions are becoming more prevalent to protect cloud infrastructure.

Intrusion Detection Systems are indispensable tools in the cybersecurity arsenal, providing organizations with the ability to detect and respond to a wide range of cyber threats. As cyber threats continue to evolve in sophistication, IDS systems are adapting with advanced technologies and strategies to provide robust protection for digital assets and networks.

B. Penetration Testing: Probing for Security Weaknesses

Penetration testing, often referred to as "pen testing," is a proactive and systematic approach to evaluating the security of an organization's digital assets and infrastructure. It involves simulating real-world cyberattacks to identify vulnerabilities, weaknesses, and potential exploits before malicious actors can capitalize on them. In this in-depth exploration, we will delve into the world of penetration testing, examining its methodologies, benefits, challenges, and the pivotal role it plays in fortifying cybersecurity defenses.

1. Introduction to Penetration Testing:

1.1. Definition:

- **Penetration Testing:** Penetration testing is a controlled and authorized process of attempting to exploit vulnerabilities in a system or network to assess its security posture.

1.2. Objectives:

- **Identify Vulnerabilities:** Discover and document security weaknesses that could be exploited by cyber adversaries.

- **Assess Risk:** Determine the potential impact and likelihood of successful cyberattacks.

2. Methodologies of Penetration Testing:

2.1. Black Box Testing:

- **Black Box Testing:** Testers have no prior knowledge of the system or network being tested, simulating an outsider's perspective.

2.2. White Box Testing:

- **White Box Testing:** Testers have full knowledge of the system's internal workings and code, simulating an insider's perspective.

2.3. Gray Box Testing:

- **Gray Box Testing:** Testers have partial knowledge of the system, typically focusing on specific areas of interest.

2.4. Types of Penetration Testing:

- **Network Penetration Testing:** Focuses on assessing vulnerabilities in network infrastructure, including firewalls, routers, and switches.

- **Web Application Penetration Testing:** Evaluates the security of web applications, including web services and APIs.

- **Wireless Penetration Testing:** Assesses the security of wireless networks and devices.

- **Social Engineering Testing:** Evaluates the susceptibility of employees to social engineering attacks.

3. Penetration Testing Process:

3.1. Planning and Scoping:

- Define the objectives, scope, and rules of engagement for the penetration test.

3.2. Information Gathering:

- Collect information about the target system or network, including IP addresses, domain names, and technologies in use.

3.3. Vulnerability Analysis:

- Identify and analyze potential vulnerabilities, including software weaknesses and misconfigurations.

3.4. Exploitation:

- Attempt to exploit identified vulnerabilities to gain unauthorized access or control.

3.5. Reporting:

- Document findings, including vulnerabilities discovered, exploitation details, and recommendations for remediation.

4. Benefits of Penetration Testing:

4.1. Security Assurance:

- Penetration testing provides organizations with confidence in their cybersecurity defenses by identifying weaknesses.

4.2. Risk Reduction:

- By addressing vulnerabilities proactively, organizations can reduce the risk of cyberattacks and data breaches.

4.3. Compliance:

- Many regulatory frameworks require regular penetration testing to ensure compliance.

5. Challenges of Penetration Testing:

5.1. Legal and Ethical Considerations:

- Penetration testing must be conducted with proper authorization to avoid legal issues.

5.2. False Positives:

- Testers must differentiate between actual vulnerabilities and false positives to avoid unnecessary remediation efforts.

5.3. Scope Limitations:

- The scope of penetration testing may not cover all potential attack vectors, leaving some vulnerabilities undiscovered.

6. Emerging Trends in Penetration Testing:

- **Automated Penetration Testing:** Machine learning and artificial intelligence are being integrated into penetration testing tools to automate certain tasks and enhance testing accuracy.

- **Cloud Penetration Testing:** As organizations migrate to the cloud, penetration testing is adapting to evaluate the security of cloud-based infrastructure and services.

7. Use Cases:

7.1. Corporate Networks:

- Organizations conduct penetration testing on their internal and external networks to ensure the security of corporate assets.

7.2. Web Applications:

- Penetration testing of web applications is crucial to prevent data breaches and protect customer information.

Penetration testing is an indispensable element of a robust cybersecurity strategy, helping organizations proactively identify and address vulnerabilities before they can be exploited by malicious actors. As cyber threats continue to evolve, penetration testing methodologies and tools adapt to provide comprehensive security assessments that strengthen an organization's cyber defenses.

C. Advanced Threat Mitigation: Defending Against Evolving Cyber Threats

Advanced Threat Mitigation encompasses a multifaceted approach to safeguarding digital assets and data against sophisticated and evolving cyber threats. These threats, which include zero-day vulnerabilities, advanced persistent threats (APTs), and nation-state actors, demand proactive and adaptive security measures. In this comprehensive exploration, we will delve into the world of advanced threat mitigation, examining its strategies, technologies, and best practices to fortify cybersecurity defenses.

1. Introduction to Advanced Threat Mitigation:

1.1. Definition:

- **Advanced Threat Mitigation:** Advanced Threat Mitigation refers to a proactive and adaptive cybersecurity approach aimed at identifying, preventing, and mitigating advanced and persistent cyber threats.

1.2. Key Objectives:

- **Early Detection:** Identify threats at the earliest stages to prevent or minimize damage.

- **Rapid Response:** Enable swift and effective responses to thwart ongoing threats.

2. Strategies for Advanced Threat Mitigation:

2.1. Threat Intelligence:

- **Threat Intelligence Feeds:** Subscribe to threat intelligence feeds that provide real-time information on emerging threats.

- **Indicators of Compromise (IoC):** Monitor IoCs to identify potential breaches.

2.2. Zero Trust Architecture:

- **Zero Trust:** Implement a Zero Trust security model where trust is never assumed, and verification is required from anyone trying to access resources in the network.

2.3. Behavioral Analytics:

- **User and Entity Behavior Analytics (UEBA):** Use UEBA to detect anomalies in user and entity behavior that may indicate compromise.

2.4. Endpoint Detection and Response (EDR):

- **EDR Solutions:** Deploy EDR solutions to monitor and respond to suspicious activities on endpoints.

2.5. Network Segmentation:

- **Micro-Segmentation:** Implement micro-segmentation to limit lateral movement of attackers within the network.

3. Technologies for Advanced Threat Mitigation:

3.1. Next-Generation Firewalls:

- **NGFWs:** Next-generation firewalls provide advanced threat detection and prevention capabilities, including intrusion detection and malware scanning.

3.2. Deception Technology:

- **Deception:** Deception technology deploys decoy resources to mislead and detect attackers within the network.

3.3. Sandboxing:

- **Sandboxing:** Sandboxes isolate and analyze suspicious files or applications in a controlled environment to detect malware.

3.4. Threat Hunting:

- **Threat Hunting Platforms:** Use threat hunting platforms to actively seek out and identify hidden threats within the network.

4. Best Practices for Advanced Threat Mitigation:

4.1. Continuous Monitoring:

- Implement continuous monitoring to detect and respond to threats in real-time.

4.2. Security Awareness Training:

- Train employees and end-users to recognize and report potential threats and phishing attempts.

4.3. Incident Response Plan:

- Develop a well-defined incident response plan that outlines actions to be taken in the event of a security breach.

5. Challenges of Advanced Threat Mitigation:

5.1. Evolving Threat Landscape:

- Threats constantly evolve, making it challenging to stay ahead of attackers.

5.2. Resource Intensive:

- Implementing advanced threat mitigation strategies can be resource-intensive, requiring investments in technology and skilled personnel.

5.3. False Positives:

- Overly aggressive security measures can lead to false positives, potentially disrupting legitimate operations.

6. Use Cases:

6.1. Enterprises and Organizations:

- Enterprises and organizations of all sizes implement advanced threat mitigation strategies to protect sensitive data and maintain business continuity.

6.2. Critical Infrastructure:

- Sectors such as energy, healthcare, and finance deploy advanced threat mitigation solutions to safeguard critical infrastructure.

As cyber threats grow in complexity and frequency, advanced threat mitigation strategies and technologies are essential for organizations seeking to protect their digital assets and data. By adopting a proactive and adaptive approach, businesses can bolster their cybersecurity defenses and effectively defend against emerging threats in an ever-evolving digital landscape.

CHAPTER 13

Hybrid Cloud and Multi-Cloud Management: Navigating the Future of Cloud Computing

Hybrid cloud and multi-cloud environments have emerged as transformative paradigms in cloud computing, offering organizations unprecedented flexibility, scalability, and resilience. This introductory exploration delves into the realms of hybrid cloud and multi-cloud management, elucidating their significance, key concepts, and the pivotal role they play in shaping the future of cloud infrastructure and services.

A. Strategies for Hybrid Cloud Deployments: Bridging On-Premises and Cloud Worlds

Hybrid cloud deployments have gained prominence as a strategic approach to cloud computing, offering organizations the flexibility to combine on-premises infrastructure with cloud resources. This approach allows businesses to optimize their IT environments for cost efficiency, scalability, and resilience. In this in-depth exploration, we will delve into the strategies for hybrid cloud deployments, examining the key considerations, benefits, challenges, and best practices for successfully integrating on-premises and cloud infrastructure.

343

Mastering IT Infrastructure Management

1. Introduction to Hybrid Cloud Deployments:

1.1. Definition:

- **Hybrid Cloud:** A hybrid cloud is a computing environment that combines on-premises infrastructure (private cloud) with one or more public cloud providers, allowing data and workloads to be shared between them.

1.2. Objectives:

- **Flexibility:** Achieve flexibility by dynamically scaling resources based on workload demands.

- **Cost Efficiency:** Optimize costs by leveraging public cloud resources when needed, avoiding overprovisioning.

2. Strategies for Hybrid Cloud Deployments:

2.1. Lift and Shift:

- **Lift and Shift:** Migrate existing on-premises applications to the cloud with minimal modifications. This approach is often used to quickly move workloads to the cloud.

2.2. Cloud Bursting:

- **Cloud Bursting:** Automatically allocate additional resources from the public cloud during peak demand, maintaining a baseline on-premises.

2.3. Data Synchronization:

- **Data Synchronization:** Implement mechanisms to synchronize data between on-premises and cloud environments, ensuring consistency.

2.4. Disaster Recovery:

- **Disaster Recovery (DR):** Use the cloud as a DR site, replicating critical data and applications to the cloud for rapid recovery.

2.5. Multi-Cloud Strategy:

- **Multi-Cloud:** Embrace a multi-cloud strategy by utilizing multiple public cloud providers for different workloads, avoiding vendor lock-in.

3. Benefits of Hybrid Cloud Deployments:

3.1. Scalability:

- Easily scale resources up or down to meet changing demands, avoiding resource constraints.

3.2. Cost Optimization:

- Optimize costs by using cloud resources on a pay-as-you-go basis and avoiding the capital expenses of on-premises infrastructure.

3.3. Geographic Redundancy:

- Ensure high availability and disaster recovery with data and applications distributed across multiple locations.

4. Challenges of Hybrid Cloud Deployments:

4.1. Integration Complexity:

- Integrating on-premises and cloud environments can be complex, requiring compatibility and connectivity considerations.

4.2. Data Security and Compliance:

- Ensuring data security and regulatory compliance across hybrid environments can be challenging.

4.3. Skill Requirements:

- IT staff may need training and expertise in both on-premises and cloud technologies.

5. Best Practices for Hybrid Cloud Deployments:

5.1. Comprehensive Strategy:

- Develop a comprehensive hybrid cloud strategy that aligns with business objectives and IT capabilities.

5.2. Security Focus:

- Prioritize security measures, including encryption, access controls, and compliance monitoring.

5.3. Automation:

- Implement automation for resource provisioning, scaling, and management to optimize efficiency.

6. Use Cases:

6.1. Enterprises:

- Large enterprises leverage hybrid cloud to maintain legacy applications on-premises while adopting cloud-native technologies for new initiatives.

6.2. E-commerce:

- E-commerce platforms use cloud bursting during high-traffic sales events to ensure performance and availability.

Hybrid cloud deployments offer organizations the best of both worlds, combining the reliability of on-premises infrastructure with the agility and scalability of the cloud. By implementing effective strategies, addressing challenges, and adhering to best practices, businesses can harness the power of hybrid cloud computing to drive innovation, improve cost efficiency, and enhance their overall IT capabilities.

B. Challenges of Multi-Cloud Management: Navigating Complexity in a Multi-Cloud World

Multi-cloud environments, where organizations leverage multiple cloud service providers simultaneously, have become increasingly popular due to their potential for flexibility, redundancy, and cost optimization. However, managing multiple clouds presents a unique set of challenges that require careful consideration and planning. In this in-depth exploration, we will delve into the challenges of multi-cloud management, examining the complexities, risks, and strategies for effectively navigating a multi-cloud landscape.

1. Introduction to Multi-Cloud Management:

1.1. Definition:

- **Multi-Cloud:** Multi-cloud refers to the use of multiple cloud service providers to host different workloads or services. This approach offers redundancy, flexibility, and the ability to select the best cloud platform for specific needs.

1.2. Objectives:

- **Flexibility:** Gain the ability to choose the most suitable cloud provider for various workloads or applications.

- **Risk Mitigation:** Reduce the risk of downtime or data loss by spreading resources across multiple clouds.

2. Challenges of Multi-Cloud Management:

2.1. Complexity:

- **Management Complexity:** Orchestrating resources, applications, and services across different cloud providers can be highly complex and challenging.

2.2. Interoperability:

- **Lack of Standardization:** Cloud providers may use proprietary technologies, making interoperability between clouds difficult.

2.3. Data Governance:

- **Data Security and Compliance:** Ensuring data security, compliance, and governance across multiple clouds can be complex and require a consistent approach.

2.4. Cost Management:

- **Cost Visibility:** Managing and optimizing costs across multiple clouds can be challenging without clear visibility and cost-tracking tools.

2.5. Skill Shortages:

- **Diverse Skill Sets:** IT teams must possess diverse skills to effectively manage and troubleshoot issues in various cloud environments.

3. Strategies for Addressing Multi-Cloud Challenges:

3.1. Cloud Management Platforms (CMPs):

- **CMPs:** Utilize cloud management platforms that provide centralized management, monitoring, and automation capabilities across multi-cloud environments.

3.2. Interoperability Standards:

- **Standardization Efforts:** Encourage cloud providers to adopt interoperability standards to ease integration challenges.

3.3. Governance and Compliance Tools:

- **Governance Tools:** Implement governance and compliance tools that offer consistent policies and controls across clouds.

3.4. Cost Optimization Solutions:

- **Cost Optimization Tools:** Use cloud cost management tools to monitor expenses, identify cost-saving opportunities, and optimize resource allocation.

3.5. Training and Skill Development:

- **Training Programs:** Invest in training and skill development for IT teams to ensure proficiency in managing diverse cloud environments.

4. Benefits of Multi-Cloud Management:

4.1. Vendor Diversification:

- **Reduced Vendor Lock-In:** Multi-cloud environments reduce dependence on a single cloud provider, minimizing vendor lock-in.

4.2. Geographic Redundancy:

- **High Availability:** Multi-cloud setups offer geographic redundancy, ensuring availability in the event of regional outages.

4.3. Application Optimization:

- **Best-Fit Services:** Select the most suitable cloud services for specific applications or workloads to optimize performance and costs.

5. Use Cases:

5.1. E-commerce Platforms:

- E-commerce platforms use multi-cloud to ensure high availability during peak shopping seasons while optimizing costs during off-peak times.

5.2. Healthcare Providers:

- Healthcare organizations utilize multi-cloud for data storage, patient records management, and compliance across various cloud providers.

Effectively managing a multi-cloud environment demands careful planning, ongoing monitoring, and a commitment to addressing the unique challenges it presents. While multi-cloud environments offer numerous advantages, organizations must remain vigilant in addressing complexity, ensuring interoperability, and maintaining strong governance to reap the benefits of a multi-cloud strategy.

CHAPTER 14

DevOps Integration: Bridging the Gap Between Development and Operations

DevOps Integration represents a cultural and technical approach that brings together development (Dev) and IT operations (Ops) teams to streamline software development, delivery, and deployment processes. This introductory exploration delves into the significance of DevOps integration, highlighting its key principles, benefits, and its transformative impact on modern software development practices.

A. DevOps Principles and Practices: Cultivating Collaboration for Efficient Software Delivery

DevOps, a portmanteau of "development" and "operations," is a cultural and technical movement that revolutionizes the way software is developed, tested, and delivered. DevOps principles and practices aim to break down silos between development and operations teams, fostering collaboration and automation to accelerate software delivery while maintaining high quality and reliability. In this in-depth exploration, we will delve into the core principles and key practices that underpin the DevOps philosophy.

353

1. Introduction to DevOps Principles and Practices:

1.1. Definition:

- **DevOps:** DevOps is a cultural and technical movement that emphasizes collaboration, automation, and continuous integration and delivery (CI/CD) to streamline software development and operations.

1.2. Objectives:

- **Faster Delivery:** Accelerate the development and deployment of software to meet business demands and market competition.

- **Reliability:** Ensure software is reliable and stable in production environments.

2. Core DevOps Principles:

2.1. Collaboration:

- **Collaborative Culture:** Foster a culture of collaboration and shared responsibility between development and operations teams.

2.2. Automation:

- **Automation:** Automate repetitive tasks and processes, such as code testing and deployment, to reduce errors and save time.

2.3. Continuous Integration and Continuous Deployment (CI/CD):

- **CI/CD Pipeline:** Implement a CI/CD pipeline to automate code integration, testing, and deployment, ensuring frequent and reliable releases.

2.4. Monitoring and Feedback:

- **Real-time Monitoring:** Continuously monitor applications and infrastructure in production to detect issues early and gather user feedback.

2.5. Infrastructure as Code (IaC):

- **IaC:** Treat infrastructure provisioning and configuration as code, enabling automated and version-controlled infrastructure management.

3. Key DevOps Practices:

3.1. Version Control:

- **Git:** Use version control systems like Git to manage and track changes in code collaboratively.

3.2. Automated Testing:

- **Unit, Integration, and Functional Testing:** Implement automated testing at different levels of the application to catch defects early.

3.3. Continuous Integration (CI):

- **CI Servers:** Employ CI servers like Jenkins or Travis CI to automatically build, test, and validate code changes as they are committed.

3.4. Continuous Deployment (CD):

- **Deployment Pipelines:** Set up deployment pipelines to automate the release of tested code changes into production.

3.5. Infrastructure Automation:

- **Configuration Management Tools:** Use tools like Ansible or Puppet to automate server provisioning and configuration.

3.6. Containerization and Orchestration:

- **Docker and Kubernetes:** Containerize applications and use orchestration tools to manage container deployments at scale.

3.7. Collaboration Tools:

- **ChatOps and Collaboration Platforms:** Utilize collaboration tools like Slack or Microsoft Teams to facilitate communication and collaboration.

4. Benefits of DevOps Principles and Practices:

4.1. Faster Time to Market:

- DevOps accelerates the software development and release cycle, allowing businesses to respond quickly to market demands.

4.2. Improved Quality:

- Automation and continuous testing lead to higher software quality and fewer production defects.

4.3. Enhanced Collaboration:

- DevOps fosters collaboration, breaking down silos between teams and promoting shared goals and responsibility.

5. Challenges of DevOps Implementation:

5.1. Cultural Resistance:

- Overcoming cultural resistance to change can be a significant challenge when implementing DevOps practices.

5.2. Tool Complexity:

- The multitude of DevOps tools and technologies can be overwhelming, requiring careful selection and integration.

5.3. Skill Requirements:

- DevOps demands a combination of development and operations skills, necessitating training and upskilling.

6. Use Cases:

6.1. E-commerce Platforms:

- E-commerce platforms use DevOps practices to ensure frequent updates, minimize downtime, and improve the shopping experience.

6.2. Software as a Service (SaaS) Providers:

- SaaS providers employ DevOps to deliver and maintain cloud-based services reliably and efficiently.

DevOps principles and practices have become integral to modern software development, enabling organizations to deliver software faster, more reliably, and with higher quality. By embracing collaboration, automation, and a culture of continuous improvement, DevOps transforms traditional development and operations into a unified and efficient process that meets the demands of today's fast-paced digital world.

B. Automation and Collaboration in DevOps: Streamlining Efficiency and Accelerating

Software Delivery

Automation and collaboration lie at the heart of DevOps, representing two essential pillars that drive the efficiency, speed, and success of software development and delivery. In this in-depth exploration, we will delve into the critical role of automation and collaboration within the DevOps framework, understanding how they work in tandem to streamline processes, reduce errors, and accelerate the deployment of high-quality software.

1. The Significance of Automation in DevOps:

1.1. Streamlining Repetitive Tasks:

- Automation in DevOps is primarily focused on automating repetitive, manual tasks throughout the software development and deployment lifecycle. This includes tasks such as code compilation, testing, deployment, and infrastructure provisioning.

1.2. Benefits of Automation:

- Automation enhances efficiency by reducing the risk of human error, shortening development and deployment cycles, and ensuring consistency in processes. It also frees up valuable human resources for more creative and complex tasks.

1.3. Key Automation Areas:

- Automation is applied across various aspects of DevOps, including code integration, testing, configuration management, deployment, and monitoring. For instance, CI/CD pipelines automate code integration, testing, and deployment, while infrastructure as code (IaC) automates server provisioning and configuration.

2. The Role of Collaboration in DevOps:

2.1. Breaking Down Silos:

- Collaboration is a fundamental cultural shift in DevOps that emphasizes the breaking down of silos between traditionally separate development and operations teams. It encourages cross-functional collaboration and shared responsibility.

2.2. Benefits of Collaboration:

- Collaboration fosters a culture of transparency, communication, and teamwork. It leads to faster issue resolution, better problem-solving, and a more holistic view of the software development and delivery process.

2.3. Key Collaboration Practices:

- Collaboration in DevOps involves practices such as cross-functional teams, shared toolchains, and collaborative decision-making. ChatOps, a practice that integrates chat and collaboration tools into the development workflow, is also gaining prominence.

3. Automation and Collaboration in Harmony:

3.1. Integration of Automation and Collaboration:

- The synergy between automation and collaboration in DevOps is profound. Automation tools and processes streamline the repetitive aspects of development and operations, while collaboration practices ensure that teams work cohesively, share insights, and make informed decisions.

3.2. Collaboration Enhances Automation:

- Collaboration fosters a culture where automation tools and practices are collectively adopted and continuously improved. Teams collaborate to define automation requirements, select appropriate tools, and refine automated workflows based on real-world experiences.

3.3. Continuous Feedback Loop:

- Automation generates valuable data and metrics, such as test results and deployment success rates. Collaboration ensures that this data is shared and discussed among team members, leading to data-driven decisions and continuous improvement.

4. DevOps Tools and Technologies:

4.1. Automation Tools:

- Automation tools in DevOps include Jenkins, Travis CI, Ansible, Puppet, and Docker for CI/CD, configuration management, and containerization.

4.2. Collaboration Tools:

- Collaboration tools include Slack, Microsoft Teams, and Atlassian's Jira and Confluence, which facilitate real-time communication and document sharing among teams.

5. Use Cases:

5.1. Cloud Service Providers:

- Cloud service providers leverage automation and collaboration to manage vast data centers efficiently and collaborate on infrastructure provisioning and monitoring.

5.2. Software Development Companies:

- Software development companies employ automation and collaboration to streamline the development process, automate testing, and ensure cross-functional communication among development, testing, and operations teams.

Automation and collaboration are the twin engines that power the DevOps journey, allowing organizations to transform their software development and delivery processes. By embracing automation to eliminate manual bottlenecks and promoting a culture of collaboration, DevOps teams can achieve not only faster and more reliable software releases but also improved teamwork and innovation across the organization.

C. DevOps Agility in Infrastructure Management: Paving the Way for Dynamic IT Operations

DevOps principles extend beyond software development and deployment; they also revolutionize the way IT infrastructure is managed. DevOps agility in infrastructure management emphasizes flexibility, scalability, and automation to meet the ever-changing demands of modern businesses. In this in-depth exploration, we will delve into the concept of DevOps agility in infrastructure management, understanding how it transforms traditional IT operations into a dynamic and responsive ecosystem.

1. Introduction to DevOps Agility in Infrastructure Management:

1.1. Definition:

- **DevOps Agility in Infrastructure Management:** This

concept embodies the application of DevOps principles to the management of IT infrastructure. It emphasizes rapid provisioning, scaling, and automation to support dynamic application needs.

1.2. Objectives:

- **Flexibility:** Enable IT infrastructure to scale up or down rapidly in response to changing workloads and demands.

- **Efficiency:** Streamline infrastructure management through automation to reduce manual intervention and errors.

2. Key Tenets of DevOps Agility in Infrastructure Management:

2.1. Infrastructure as Code (IaC):

- **IaC:** Treat infrastructure provisioning and configuration as code, allowing for automated and version-controlled infrastructure management. Tools like Terraform and Ansible are commonly used for IaC.

2.2. Continuous Integration and Continuous Deployment (CI/CD):

- **CI/CD Pipelines:** Implement CI/CD pipelines not only for application code but also for infrastructure changes, enabling automated testing and deployment of infrastructure updates.

2.3. Automation and Orchestration:

- **Automation Tools:** Leverage automation and orchestration tools to automate routine infrastructure tasks, such as server provisioning, configuration, and scaling.

2.4. Monitoring and Feedback Loop:

- **Real-time Monitoring:** Continuously monitor infrastructure components to detect and respond to performance issues and resource constraints in real-time.

3. DevOps Agility in Action:

3.1. Rapid Infrastructure Provisioning:

- DevOps enables the quick provisioning of infrastructure resources, allowing teams to create and tear down environments on-demand, reducing lead times for development and testing.

3.2. Scalability:

- DevOps agility ensures that infrastructure can scale horizontally or vertically to accommodate varying workloads, from development and testing to production.

3.3. Self-service Portals:

- Self-service portals and dashboards empower development

and operations teams to request and manage infrastructure resources independently, reducing administrative overhead.

3.4. Rollback Capabilities:

- In case of issues or failures, DevOps practices facilitate easy rollback to a previous infrastructure state, minimizing downtime and impact on users.

4. Challenges of DevOps Agility in Infrastructure Management:

4.1. Cultural Shift:

- Implementing DevOps in infrastructure management requires a cultural shift, with teams accustomed to traditional practices needing to embrace automation and collaboration.

4.2. Skill Requirements:

- Infrastructure teams may need to acquire new skills in areas like scripting, IaC, and CI/CD.

4.3. Tooling and Integration:

- Selecting and integrating the right tools for infrastructure automation and orchestration can be complex, requiring careful planning.

5. Use Cases:

5.1. Cloud Providers:

- Cloud service providers leverage DevOps agility to offer scalable and automated infrastructure services to customers.

5.2. Enterprises:

- Enterprises adopt DevOps agility in infrastructure management to optimize resource allocation, reduce operational costs, and enhance the scalability of their IT environments.

DevOps agility in infrastructure management is the driving force behind the transformation of IT operations. By treating infrastructure as code, automating routine tasks, and fostering a culture of collaboration, organizations can ensure that their IT infrastructure is not a bottleneck but a dynamic, responsive, and efficient resource that aligns with the needs of the business.

CHAPTER 15

Comprehensive Case Studies: Real-World Insights into IT Infrastructure Management

Comprehensive case studies provide invaluable insights into the practical application of IT infrastructure management principles and best practices in real-world scenarios. In this introductory exploration, we will set the stage for an in-depth examination of comprehensive case studies, highlighting their importance in showcasing effective infrastructure management strategies, industry-specific challenges, and successful solutions employed by organizations across various sectors.

A. Real-world Examples of Effective IT Infrastructure Management: Learning from Success Stories

Effective IT infrastructure management is the linchpin of modern organizations' operations, enabling them to deliver services, ensure security, and remain competitive in the digital age. To gain a deeper understanding of best practices and strategies, it is essential to examine real-world examples of successful IT infrastructure management. In this in-depth exploration, we will delve into compelling case studies that highlight how organizations have effectively managed their IT infrastructure to achieve operational excellence and drive business success.

1. Case Study: Netflix - Streaming Success with Cloud-Based Infrastructure:

1.1. Background:

- Netflix, the global streaming giant, shifted from a traditional data center-based infrastructure to a cloud-based model, primarily using Amazon Web Services (AWS).

1.2. Key Strategies and Outcomes:

- **Scalability:** Leveraging AWS's scalability, Netflix can handle massive concurrent user loads, especially during peak viewing hours.

- **Redundancy:** Netflix's infrastructure spans multiple AWS regions, ensuring redundancy and high availability.

- **Content Delivery:** To optimize content delivery, Netflix developed its Content Delivery Network (CDN), Open Connect, to reduce latency and improve streaming quality.

1.3. Takeaways:

- Netflix's success demonstrates the advantages of cloud-based infrastructure, scalability, redundancy, and strategic content delivery in the media streaming industry.

2. Case Study: Spotify - Microservices Architecture for Scalability:

2.1. Background:

- Spotify, the music streaming service, adopted a microservices architecture to manage its growing user base and complex infrastructure.

2.2. Key Strategies and Outcomes:

- **Microservices:** Spotify's architecture divides its application into small, independently deployable microservices, enabling rapid development, scalability, and fault isolation.

- **Decentralized Teams:** Each microservice has a dedicated team responsible for its development and operation, promoting ownership and accountability.

- **Continuous Deployment:** Spotify uses CI/CD pipelines for automated testing and deployment, ensuring a steady flow of updates to its platform.

2.3. Takeaways:

- Spotify's adoption of microservices showcases how a modular and decentralized approach can support scalability, rapid development, and reliability in a fast-paced industry.

3. Case Study: Delta Airlines - IT Resilience for Business Continuity:

3.1. Background:

- Delta Airlines, a major airline carrier, invested in robust IT infrastructure and disaster recovery solutions to ensure business continuity.

3.2. Key Strategies and Outcomes:

- **Data Centers and Redundancy:** Delta maintains multiple data centers with redundant systems to prevent downtime and data loss.

- **Disaster Recovery Testing:** Regular testing of disaster recovery procedures ensures readiness for unexpected events.

- **Cloud Integration:** Delta uses cloud solutions to offload non-essential workloads, reducing the risk of capacity-related disruptions.

3.3. Takeaways:

- Delta's commitment to IT resilience and disaster recovery demonstrates the importance of infrastructure preparedness and continuity planning in the airline industry.

4. Case Study: Walmart - Data Center Optimization for Cost Savings:

4.1. Background:

- Walmart, the retail giant, embarked on a data center optimization journey to reduce costs and improve energy efficiency.

4.2. Key Strategies and Outcomes:

- **Consolidation:** Walmart reduced the number of data centers, optimizing resource utilization and energy consumption.

- **Virtualization:** Extensive server virtualization increased hardware efficiency and reduced the physical footprint of data centers.

- **Renewable Energy:** Walmart committed to using renewable energy sources to power its data centers, reducing its carbon footprint.

4.3. Takeaways:

- Walmart's data center optimization exemplifies the economic and environmental benefits of efficient infrastructure management in the retail sector.

These real-world case studies illustrate how effective IT infrastructure management strategies align with organizational goals and industry-specific challenges. Whether it's adopting cloud-based infrastructure, embracing microservices, ensuring business continuity, or optimizing data centers, these examples provide valuable lessons for organizations seeking to enhance their infrastructure management practices and achieve success in today's competitive landscape.

B. Industry-specific Case Studies: Tailoring IT Infrastructure Management for Success

In the realm of IT infrastructure management, one size does not fit all. Different industries face unique challenges and opportunities that require tailored approaches to infrastructure management. Industry-specific case studies offer valuable insights into how organizations within various sectors optimize their IT infrastructure to drive efficiency, security, and competitive advantage. In this in-depth exploration, we will delve into industry-specific case studies that showcase how businesses across different domains leverage IT infrastructure to achieve their objectives.

1. Healthcare: Case Study on Epic Systems - Optimizing IT Infrastructure for Patient Care:

1.1. Background:

- Epic Systems, a leading electronic health record (EHR)

software provider, serves healthcare organizations globally. Maintaining a highly available and secure infrastructure is critical to support healthcare delivery.

1.2. Key Strategies and Outcomes:

- **High Availability:** Epic Systems' infrastructure prioritizes high availability to ensure that EHR systems are accessible 24/7, minimizing downtime in healthcare settings.

- **Security and Compliance:** Stringent security measures and compliance with regulations like HIPAA (Health Insurance Portability and Accountability Act) safeguard patient data.

- **Scalability:** As healthcare facilities grow, Epic Systems' infrastructure can scale to accommodate increasing data and user demands.

1.3. Takeaways:

- Healthcare organizations must prioritize the reliability, security, and scalability of their IT infrastructure to provide seamless patient care and meet regulatory requirements.

2. Finance: Case Study on JPMorgan Chase - Resilient Infrastructure for Financial Transactions:

2.1. Background:

- JPMorgan Chase, a global financial institution, relies on a robust IT infrastructure to support financial transactions, trading, and customer services.

2.2. Key Strategies and Outcomes:

- **Redundancy and Disaster Recovery:** Multiple data centers with redundancy ensure uninterrupted service, even in the face of system failures.

- **Low Latency:** Ultra-low latency infrastructure is crucial for high-frequency trading operations.

- **Security and Compliance:** JPMorgan Chase maintains rigorous security measures and compliance with financial industry regulations to protect customer assets.

2.3. Takeaways:

- In the finance sector, IT infrastructure resilience, low latency, and security are paramount to ensure the integrity of financial operations and customer trust.

3. Manufacturing: Case Study on Toyota - IoT-Enabled Infrastructure for Production Efficiency:

3.1. Background:

- Toyota, a pioneer in lean manufacturing, leverages IT infrastructure to optimize production processes, quality control, and supply chain management.

3.2. Key Strategies and Outcomes:

- **Internet of Things (IoT):** Toyota uses IoT sensors to collect real-time data from manufacturing equipment, enabling predictive maintenance and reducing downtime.

- **Inventory Management:** IT infrastructure supports inventory optimization and just-in-time manufacturing to reduce costs.

- **Data Analytics:** Advanced analytics on manufacturing data help identify process improvements and quality control measures.

3.3. Takeaways:

- In manufacturing, IT infrastructure can enhance operational efficiency, quality control, and supply chain management, contributing to cost reduction and product quality.

4. Retail: Case Study on Amazon - Scalable Cloud Infrastructure for E-commerce:

4.1. Background:

- Amazon, one of the world's largest e-commerce platforms, relies on a scalable and agile cloud infrastructure to support its vast online retail operations.

4.2. Key Strategies and Outcomes:

- **Amazon Web Services (AWS):** Amazon's own cloud service, AWS, provides the scalable infrastructure required to handle massive traffic spikes during peak shopping seasons.

- **Personalization:** Amazon uses customer data and AI algorithms to provide personalized product recommendations, requiring a robust infrastructure for data processing.

- **Supply Chain Optimization:** IT infrastructure supports efficient order fulfillment and supply chain management, ensuring fast delivery.

4.3. Takeaways:

- In the retail sector, scalable cloud infrastructure, data-driven personalization, and supply chain optimization are critical to success in the competitive e-commerce landscape.

These industry-specific case studies exemplify the importance of tailoring IT infrastructure management strategies to meet the unique needs and challenges of different sectors. Whether it's ensuring high availability in healthcare, resilience in finance, efficiency in manufacturing, or scalability in retail, organizations can draw inspiration from these examples to optimize their IT infrastructure and drive success in their respective industries.

C. Challenges Faced and Overcome in IT Infrastructure Management

Effective IT infrastructure management is crucial for organizations to thrive in today's digital landscape. However, it comes with its fair share of challenges. In this in-depth exploration, we will delve into the common challenges faced by IT infrastructure management teams and how they are overcome through innovative solutions and best practices.

1. Challenge: Legacy Systems and Technical Debt

- **Description:** Many organizations still rely on legacy systems, which are outdated and challenging to maintain. Technical debt, accrued through shortcuts and quick fixes, can impede system modernization efforts.

- **Overcoming the Challenge:**

    - **Gradual Modernization:** Organizations adopt a phased approach to modernize legacy systems, gradually migrating to more scalable and efficient technologies.

    - **Refactoring and Cleanup:** Addressing technical debt through code refactoring and cleanup reduces long-term maintenance costs.

2. Challenge: Scalability and Performance

- **Description:** As businesses grow, IT infrastructure must scale to accommodate increased workloads and user demands. Ensuring consistent performance can be challenging.

- **Overcoming the Challenge:**

  - **Cloud Adoption:** Leveraging cloud services allows for elastic scalability, with resources provisioned as needed.

  - **Load Balancing:** Load balancers distribute traffic evenly across servers, optimizing performance.

3. Challenge: Security Threats

- **Description:** Cybersecurity threats, such as data breaches and ransomware attacks, pose a significant risk to IT infrastructure.

- **Overcoming the Challenge:**

  - **Security Measures:** Implementing robust security measures, including firewalls, intrusion detection systems, and encryption, helps protect infrastructure.

  - **Regular Updates:** Keeping software and systems up to date with security patches is critical.

4. Challenge: Resource Management

- **Description:** Efficiently managing hardware and software resources to avoid underutilization or overprovisioning is a delicate balancing act.

- **Overcoming the Challenge:**

  - **Resource Monitoring:** Continuous monitoring of resource usage helps identify inefficiencies and allows for optimization.

  - **Automation:** Automation tools and scripts can dynamically allocate resources based on demand, reducing waste.

5. Challenge: Compliance and Regulations

- **Description:** Organizations must comply with various industry-specific regulations and data protection laws, which can be complex and constantly changing.

- **Overcoming the Challenge:**

  - **Regular Audits:** Conducting regular compliance audits ensures adherence to regulations.

  - **Documentation:** Comprehensive documentation of IT policies and procedures helps demonstrate compliance.

6. Challenge: Data Management and Backup

- **Description:** Safeguarding data, ensuring data integrity, and creating reliable backup systems are vital challenges.

- **Overcoming the Challenge:**

  - **Data Backup and Recovery Plans:** Implementing robust backup and recovery plans with offsite storage options ensures data availability.

  - **Data Lifecycle Management:** Developing data lifecycle management strategies helps manage data from creation to deletion.

7. Challenge: Cost Management

- **Description:** Balancing the costs of IT infrastructure with the organization's budget constraints can be challenging.

- **Overcoming the Challenge:**

  - **Cost Estimation:** Accurate cost estimation and budgeting help prevent overspending.

  - **Cloud Cost Optimization:** In cloud environments, organizations optimize costs by rightsizing resources and utilizing cost control tools.

8. Challenge: Human Resources

- **Description:** Recruiting and retaining skilled IT professionals is a challenge, especially in competitive job markets.

- **Overcoming the Challenge:**

    - **Training and Development:** Providing ongoing training and opportunities for skill development can help retain talent.

    - **Outsourcing:** In some cases, outsourcing certain IT functions to specialized providers can address resource shortages.

9. Challenge: Disaster Recovery and Business Continuity

- **Description:** Ensuring that IT infrastructure can recover swiftly from disasters and disruptions is essential.

- **Overcoming the Challenge:**

    - **Disaster Recovery Planning:** Developing comprehensive disaster recovery plans with backup data centers and failover procedures.

    - **Regular Testing:** Conducting regular disaster recovery drills ensures readiness.

10. Challenge: Change Management

- **Description:** Implementing changes to IT infrastructure, whether due to upgrades or process changes, can lead to resistance and disruption.

- **Overcoming the Challenge:**

  - **Effective Communication:** Clear and proactive communication with stakeholders helps manage expectations and reduces resistance.

  - **Change Control Processes:** Implementing change control processes ensures changes are well-documented and tested.

In conclusion, IT infrastructure management is a complex and ever-evolving field. While challenges are inevitable, organizations can overcome them through strategic planning, embracing emerging technologies, and fostering a culture of adaptability and continuous improvement. Addressing these challenges effectively ensures that IT infrastructure remains a reliable and agile foundation for business operations.

Conclusion

As we draw the final curtain on this journey through these pages, we invite you to reflect on the knowledge, insights, and discoveries that have unfolded before you. Our exploration of various subjects has been a captivating voyage into the depths of understanding.

In these chapters, we have ventured through the intricacies of numerous topics and examined the key concepts and findings that define these fields. It is our hope that you have found inspiration, enlightenment, and valuable takeaways that resonate with you on your own quest for knowledge.

Remember that the pursuit of understanding is an ever-evolving journey, and this book is but a milestone along the way. The world of knowledge is vast and boundless, offering endless opportunities for exploration and growth.

As you conclude this book, we encourage you to carry forward the torch of curiosity and continue your exploration of these subjects. Seek out new perspectives, engage in meaningful discussions, and embrace the thrill of lifelong learning.

We express our sincere gratitude for joining us on this intellectual adventure. Your curiosity and dedication to expanding your horizons are the driving forces behind our shared quest for wisdom and insight.

Thank you for entrusting us with a portion of your intellectual journey. May your pursuit of knowledge lead you to new heights and inspire others to embark on their own quests for understanding.

With sincere appreciation,

Nikhilesh Mishra, Author

Recap of Key Takeaways

In the dynamic world of IT Infrastructure Management, where technologies and best practices continually evolve, it's crucial to distill key takeaways from our comprehensive exploration. **"Mastering IT Infrastructure Management: Concepts, Techniques, and Applications"** offers a roadmap for organizations striving to construct and sustain efficient, secure, and adaptable IT infrastructures. Let's recap the essential insights:

1. **Significance of IT Infrastructure Management:**

   - IT infrastructure is foundational for modern organizations, impacting efficiency and security.

2. **Historical Evolution:**

   - Understanding historical context helps anticipate future trends in infrastructure management.

3. **Role in Modern Organizations:**

   - "Mastering IT Infrastructure Management" enables digital transformation, remote work, and enhanced customer experiences.

4. **Benefits and Challenges:**

   - Infrastructure offers scalability and efficiency benefits but also presents challenges like security threats and technical debt.

5. **Setting Objectives:**

   - Clear objectives in "Mastering IT Infrastructure Management" guide effective infrastructure management decisions and resource allocation.

6. **IT Infrastructure Components:**

   - A holistic view includes data centers, hardware, software, and networking for comprehensive management.

7. **Planning and Design:**

   - Considerations in "Mastering IT Infrastructure Management" include capacity planning, scalability, redundancy, disaster recovery, security, and budgeting.

8. **IT Service Management (ITSM):**

- ITIL principles in "Mastering IT Infrastructure Management," service catalogs, and managing incidents, problems, and changes enhance service delivery.

9. **Infrastructure as Code (IaC) and Automation:**

- IaC and automation in "Mastering IT Infrastructure Management" improve agility and reduce errors in provisioning and configuration.

10. **Networking and Data Center Setup:**

- Location, power, cooling, security, and network architecture in "Mastering IT Infrastructure Management" are vital considerations.

11. Cabling, Crimping, and Hardware Installation:

- Understanding cabling types, routing, and best practices in "Mastering IT Infrastructure Management" ensures reliable connectivity.

12. Data Center Setup and Configuration:

- Effective planning, layout, and documentation in "Mastering IT Infrastructure Management" maintain a well-functioning infrastructure.

13. Cloud Infrastructure Management:

- Understanding cloud models, deployment options, and multi-cloud strategies in "Mastering IT Infrastructure Management" is crucial in a hybrid IT landscape.

14. Storage and Data Management:

- Data storage technologies, backup, recovery, and data lifecycle management in "Mastering IT Infrastructure Management" ensure data integrity.

15. Virtualization and Containerization:

- Optimize resource utilization and support agile application deployment in "Mastering IT Infrastructure Management."

16. Advanced Security Measures:

- Intrusion detection, penetration testing, and threat mitigation in "Mastering IT Infrastructure Management" are crucial for safeguarding infrastructure.

17. Hybrid Cloud and Multi-Cloud Management:

- Strategies for hybrid cloud deployments and multi-cloud challenges in "Mastering IT Infrastructure Management" require thoughtful planning.

18. DevOps Integration:

- DevOps principles like automation and collaboration in "Mastering IT Infrastructure Management" enhance infrastructure management agility.

19. **Comprehensive Case Studies:**

- Real-world examples in "Mastering IT Infrastructure Management" illustrate successful infrastructure management approaches across industries.

20. **Industry-specific Case Studies:**

- Tailoring infrastructure management in "Mastering IT Infrastructure Management" optimizes operations and competitiveness within industries.

21. **Challenges Faced and Overcome:**

- Addressing challenges such as legacy systems, scalability, security, and resource management in "Mastering IT Infrastructure Management" requires strategic planning.

22. **The Future of IT Infrastructure Management:**

- Embracing emerging trends like hybrid and multi-cloud, edge computing, AI, and security models in "Mastering IT Infrastructure Management" is essential

Mastering IT Infrastructure Management

for navigating a dynamic future.

This comprehensive guide equips organizations with the knowledge and strategies necessary to thrive in the ever-evolving landscape of IT infrastructure management.

The Future of IT Infrastructure Management

In the rapidly evolving landscape of IT, the future of infrastructure management holds exciting prospects and significant challenges. As organizations continue to rely heavily on technology for their operations and growth, IT infrastructure management becomes a critical driver of innovation, efficiency, and competitiveness. The following key trends and considerations are shaping the future of IT infrastructure management:

1. Hybrid and Multi-Cloud Environments:

- Organizations are increasingly adopting hybrid and multi-cloud strategies to optimize resource utilization, enhance scalability, and improve disaster recovery capabilities. The future will see even more sophisticated tools and practices for managing complex cloud ecosystems.

2. Edge Computing:

- With the proliferation of IoT devices and the need for real-time data processing, edge computing is becoming integral. IT infrastructure management will need to extend to the edge, necessitating the deployment of smaller data centers and intelligent edge devices.

3. Artificial Intelligence (AI) and Machine Learning (ML):

- AI and ML are transforming infrastructure management by automating routine tasks, predicting and preventing issues, and optimizing resource allocation. The future will witness AI-driven infrastructure management platforms that can self-optimize and self-heal.

4. Security and Compliance:

- Cybersecurity threats continue to evolve, and regulatory requirements are becoming more stringent. The future of IT infrastructure management involves an increased focus on proactive threat detection, robust access controls, and compliance automation to protect critical data and systems.

5. Sustainable Practices:

- Environmental concerns are driving a shift toward sustainable IT infrastructure management. Data centers are being designed with energy efficiency in mind, and organizations are exploring renewable energy sources. Carbon footprint reduction will be a key consideration in the future.

6. Automation and DevOps Integration:

- Automation will continue to play a pivotal role, not only in provisioning and configuration but also in orchestration and policy enforcement. DevOps practices will further integrate development and operations teams, enhancing agility and collaboration.

7. Software-Defined Everything (SDx):

- SDx encompasses software-defined networking, storage, and even infrastructure management itself. It enables flexibility and adaptability, allowing IT administrators to allocate and reallocate resources dynamically.

8. Zero Trust Architecture:

- The zero trust model, where trust is never assumed and verification is continuous, will become more prevalent. This approach enhances security by minimizing the attack surface and verifying every access attempt.

9. 5G Technology:

- The rollout of 5G networks will enable faster data transmission and lower latency, opening doors to new possibilities for IoT and mobile computing. IT infrastructure management will need to accommodate the demands of this high-speed connectivity.

10. Talent and Skill Development: - As technology evolves, so too must the skill sets of IT professionals. Continuous training and development will be crucial to stay current with emerging technologies and practices in infrastructure management.

In summary, the future of IT infrastructure management is characterized by agility, intelligence, security, and sustainability.

Organizations that embrace these trends and adapt their infrastructure management strategies accordingly will be better positioned to meet the challenges and opportunities of the digital age. **"Mastering IT Infrastructure Management: Concepts, Techniques, and Applications"** provides a solid foundation for understanding and navigating this dynamic future.

Glossary of Terms

In the realm of IT Infrastructure Management, a firm grasp of the terminology and concepts is paramount to navigating the complexities of modern technology environments. "**Mastering IT Infrastructure Management: Concepts, Techniques, and Applications**" equips readers with the knowledge needed to efficiently plan, build, and maintain IT infrastructures. To aid in this journey, here's an extensive glossary of key terms:

1. **IT Infrastructure Management:**

   - The discipline of planning, designing, implementing, and maintaining the components that make up an organization's IT environment, including hardware, software, networks, and data centers.

2. **Data Center:**

   - A facility used to house and manage computer systems and associated components, such as servers, storage systems, networking equipment, and power and cooling infrastructure.

3. **Hardware Infrastructure:**

   - The physical components of an IT system, including servers, storage devices, networking equipment, and peripherals.

4. **Software Infrastructure:**

- The software components of an IT system, including operating systems, virtualization software, and middleware that enable applications to run efficiently.

5. **Network Architecture:**

- The design and structure of an organization's network, including LAN (Local Area Network), WAN (Wide Area Network), and VPN (Virtual Private Network) configurations.

6. **Cloud Infrastructure:**

- The hardware and software components in cloud computing environments, including virtual servers, storage, and networking resources.

7. **Infrastructure as Code (IaC):**

- A practice that involves automating the provisioning and management of IT infrastructure using code, allowing for agility and scalability.

8. **Scalability:**

- The ability of an IT infrastructure to handle increased workload or demand by adding resources without significant disruption.

9. **Redundancy:**

- Duplication of critical components or systems to ensure continued operation in case of failure, reducing downtime and improving reliability.

10. **Disaster Recovery:**

- A set of processes and procedures for recovering IT systems and data after a catastrophic event, ensuring business continuity.

11. **Security Considerations:**

- Measures and practices aimed at protecting IT infrastructure from unauthorized access, data breaches, and cyber threats.

12. **Capacity Planning:**

- The process of forecasting and allocating resources to meet current and future IT infrastructure demands.

13. **IT Service Management (ITSM):**

- A set of practices for designing, delivering, and managing IT services to meet the needs of the organization and its customers.

14. ITIL (Information Technology Infrastructure Library):

- A framework of best practices for ITSM that focuses on aligning IT services with the needs of the business.

15. Infrastructure Automation:

- The use of tools and scripts to automate tasks such as provisioning, configuration, and monitoring of IT infrastructure components.

16. DevOps:

- A cultural and technical approach that emphasizes collaboration between development and operations teams to automate and streamline the software delivery and infrastructure management processes.

17. Edge Computing:

- A distributed computing paradigm that brings computation and data storage closer to the data source or edge devices, reducing latency and enabling real-time processing.

18. Zero Trust Architecture:

- A security model that assumes no trust within or outside the organization's network, requiring continuous verification and strict access controls.

19. Virtualization:

- The practice of creating virtual instances of hardware or software resources, enabling greater resource utilization and flexibility.

20. Containerization:

- The use of containers to package and deploy applications and their dependencies in isolated environments, facilitating consistent deployment and scaling.

21. Intrusion Detection System (IDS):

- A security tool that monitors network traffic for suspicious activity and alerts administrators to potential security breaches.

22. Penetration Testing:

- The practice of simulating cyberattacks on an IT infrastructure to identify vulnerabilities and weaknesses that could be exploited by malicious actors.

23. Big Data:

- Large and complex datasets that require specialized tools and techniques for storage, processing, and analysis.

24. Hybrid Cloud:

- A cloud computing environment that combines private and public cloud resources to achieve greater flexibility and scalability.

25. Multi-Cloud:

- The use of multiple cloud service providers to distribute workloads and reduce vendor lock-in.

This glossary provides a comprehensive reference for understanding the terminology and concepts related to IT Infrastructure Management as discussed in your book.

Resources and References

As you reach the final pages of this book by Nikhilesh Mishra, consider it not an ending but a stepping stone. The pursuit of knowledge is an unending journey, and the world of information is boundless.

Discover a World Beyond These Pages

We extend a warm invitation to explore a realm of boundless learning and discovery through our dedicated online platform: **www.nikhileshmishra.com**. Here, you will unearth a carefully curated trove of resources and references to empower your quest for wisdom.

Unleash the Potential of Your Mind

- **Digital Libraries:** Immerse yourself in vast digital libraries, granting access to books, research papers, and academic treasures.

- **Interactive Courses:** Engage with interactive courses and lectures from world-renowned institutions, nurturing your thirst for knowledge.

- **Enlightening Talks:** Be captivated by enlightening talks delivered by visionaries and experts from diverse fields.

- **Community Connections:** Connect with a global community of like-minded seekers, engage in meaningful discussions, and share your knowledge journey.

Your Journey Has Just Begun

Your journey as a seeker of knowledge need not end here. Our website awaits your exploration, offering a gateway to an infinite universe of insights and references tailored to ignite your intellectual curiosity.

Acknowledgments

As I stand at this pivotal juncture, reflecting upon the completion of this monumental work, I am overwhelmed with profound gratitude for the exceptional individuals who have been instrumental in shaping this remarkable journey.

In Loving Memory

To my father, **Late Shri Krishna Gopal Mishra,** whose legacy of wisdom and strength continues to illuminate my path, even in his physical absence, I offer my deepest respect and heartfelt appreciation.

The Pillars of Support

My mother, **Mrs. Vijay Kanti Mishra,** embodies unwavering resilience and grace. Your steadfast support and unwavering faith in my pursuits have been the bedrock of my journey.

To my beloved wife, **Mrs. Anshika Mishra,** your unshakable belief in my abilities has been an eternal wellspring of motivation. Your constant encouragement has propelled me to reach new heights.

My daughter, **Miss Aarvi Mishra,** infuses my life with boundless joy and unbridled inspiration. Your insatiable curiosity serves as a constant reminder of the limitless power of exploration and discovery.

Brothers in Arms

To my younger brothers, **Mr. Ashutosh Mishra** and **Mr. Devashish Mishra,** who have steadfastly stood by my side, offering unwavering support and shared experiences that underscore the strength of familial bonds.

A Journey Shared

This book is a testament to the countless hours of dedication and effort that have gone into its creation. I am immensely grateful for the privilege of sharing my knowledge and insights with a global audience.

Readers, My Companions

To all the readers who embark on this intellectual journey alongside me, your curiosity and unquenchable thirst for knowledge inspire me to continually push the boundaries of understanding in the realm of cloud computing.

With profound appreciation and sincere gratitude,

Nikhilesh Mishra

September 08, 2023

About the Author

Nikhilesh Mishra is an extraordinary visionary, propelled by an insatiable curiosity and an unyielding passion for innovation. With a relentless commitment to exploring the boundaries of knowledge and technology, Nikhilesh has embarked on an exceptional journey to unravel the intricate complexities of our world.

Hailing from the vibrant and diverse landscape of India, Nikhilesh's pursuit of knowledge has driven him to plunge deep into the world of discovery and understanding from a remarkably young age. His unwavering determination and quest for innovation have not only cemented his position as a thought leader but have also earned him global recognition in the ever-evolving realm of technology and human understanding.

Over the years, Nikhilesh has not only mastered the art of translating complex concepts into accessible insights but has also crafted a unique talent for inspiring others to explore the limitless possibilities of human potential.

Nikhilesh's journey transcends the mere boundaries of expertise; it is a transformative odyssey that challenges conventional wisdom and redefines the essence of exploration. His commitment to pushing the boundaries and reimagining the norm serves as a luminous beacon of inspiration to all those who aspire to make a profound impact in the world of knowledge.

As you navigate the intricate corridors of human understanding and innovation, you will not only gain insight into Nikhilesh's expertise but also experience his unwavering dedication to empowering readers like you. Prepare to be enthralled as he seamlessly melds intricate insights with real-world applications, igniting the flames of curiosity and innovation within each reader.

Nikhilesh Mishra's work extends beyond the realm of authorship; it is a reflection of his steadfast commitment to shaping the future of knowledge and exploration. It is an embodiment of his boundless dedication to disseminating wisdom for the betterment of individuals worldwide.

Prepare to be inspired, enlightened, and empowered as you embark on this transformative journey alongside Nikhilesh Mishra. Your understanding of the world will be forever enriched, and your passion for exploration and innovation will reach new heights under his expert guidance.

Sincerely, **A Fellow Explorer**

Notes

Notes

Notes

Notes

Notes

Notes

www.ingramcontent.com/pod-product-compliance
Lightning Source LLC
LaVergne TN
LVHW052056060326
832903LV00061B/2914